LIVING WITH A GREEN HEART

How to Keep Your Body, Your Home, and the Planet Healthy in a Toxic World

GAY BROWNE

Foreword by TERRY TAMMINEN, CEO of the Leonardo DiCaprio Foundation, and former Secretary of the California EPA

Praise for *LIVING WITH A GREEN HEART*

"Veteran environmental warrior, Gay Browne's book, *Living with a Green Heart*, is both a compelling account of her evolution as an activist and a primer for aligning our diets and personal habits with the higher calling of social responsibility."
—**Robert Kennedy, Jr., Senior Attorney, Waterkeeper Alliance, author, and activist**

"If you want one of the shortest, fastest routes to getting toxic chemicals out of your life, get behind the wheel of Gay Browne's, *Living with a Green Heart* and you'll get there in no time flat."
—**Ken Cook, President, Environmental Working Group**

"Gay Browne is on a mission to help us protect ourselves, our families, and our planet. Her book challenges readers to explore the impacts our everyday choices have on ourselves and the world around us, and inspires them to take action to create a healthier future for both."
—**John H. Adams, Founding Director, Natural Resources Defense Council**

"Gay Browne's book is down-to-earth, smart, and accessible. She makes it easy for people to find information and inspiration for everyday solutions to the toxic trespass of corporate chemicals in our bodies, and in our world. Gay's advice is practical, positive and evokes the equanimity of someone who truly lives with a green heart."
—**Michael Green, CEO, Center for Environmental Health**

"Gay Browne's book invites—and challenges—each of us to do our part to create the world we want to live in, and it's filled with loads of practical ideas to do so. So stop whining and worrying, and tap into the positive energy in your own green heart! I guarantee you can make a difference!"
—**Kathy Calvin, President and CEO, United Nations Foundation**

"*Living with a Green Heart* provides valuable tools and information we can apply as individuals in order to heal the planet collectively. Gay Browne inspires us to open our hearts to live a more connected and conscious life.
—**Kelly Meyer, trustee of the Natural Resource Defense Council and co-founder of the Women's Cancer Research Fund**

"Solving the threat from climate change requires an army of environmental warriors, and Gay Browne's book is an excellent recruiting manual. Read it, share it, and join the cause while we still have time to save the planet."
—**Durwood Zaelke, Founding President, Institute for Governance & Sustainable Development, Washington DC and Paris**

"Gay Browne lives with a green heart and her new book will invite you to do so too. Accessible and practical, Gay's book will expand the possibilities of saving ourselves and healing our planet."

—Dr. Jennifer Freed, Ph.D., MFT

"It's hard to imagine a more thoughtful or more helpful book than *Living with a Green Heart*. Gay Browne speaks from her own heart and vast knowledge to focus us on what really matters for our own and our family's health, and connect that with ways we can make a difference on a much bigger scale."

—Bob Perkowitz, President, ecoAmerica

"Wondering where to start the journey to make the world and your home a better and safer place for you and your family? Look no further. Everything you need is right here in this amazing and comprehensive guide to green living. Gay Browne has provided you with the most practical and thoughtful book I've ever seen!"

—Jeffrey Hollender, Founding CEO, Seventh Generation and Sustain Natural

"As parents, we bonded over the best ways to take care of our family as well as the planet. And specifically, how to share what we learned with others in the most authentic and nonjudgmental way. With all the noise we are exposed to in the media, the need for a book that provides an honest and achievable way to live a greener and healthier lifestyle needs to be the handbook we all look to."

—Debbie Levin, CEO, Environmental Media Association

"Our planet needs advocates like Gay Browne. While the ultimate answers to planetary toxification are systemic—meaning comprehensive chemicals policy reform and a fundamental shift in the way chemicals, materials and processes are designed—Browne does us all a service by promoting consumer and individual actions that may help reduce individual risk and, most important, increase demand for safer chemistry and a less toxic world."

—Alison Carlson, President, Forsythia Foundation
and Rachel's Network member

"What a delightful read! Just the right mixture of business sense, common sense, and personal incentives! *Living with a Green Heart* is bound to align with your perspectives because ultimately we all want our immediate and long-term future to be healthy and happy. Kudos to Gay Browne!"

—Lisa Craig Gautier, President and co-founder, MatterOfTrust.org

"As someone who is wildly passionate about environmental health as a longtime board member of EWG and participant in the first intergenerational toxic body burden study, I think of myself as pretty knowledgeable on the subject. What Gay's book has done is showed me that there is so much more to learn. I am grateful to her for informing and strengthening the movement in her quest to protect us, our families, and communities."

—Laura Turner Seydel, philanthropist, Chairperson and
volunteer, Captain Planet Foundation

"Gay Browne is a Force of Nature—as is every one of us. We all make a difference. But is your overall impact healing or destructive? Are you a Consumer or a Regenerator of your life support system? Living with a Green Heart provides simple guidance to answer the questions and begin or accelerate your way to healthier and safer you—along with your home, your community, and your world."

—Andy Lipkis, Founder and President, Tree People

"A hands-on guide to green living written from a personal perspective and full of Gay's warmth, care, and compassion. A joyful reminder that we can make a difference in all our daily choices—both large and small."

—Mary Cordaro, Healthy Building and Indoor Environmental Consultant

"Whether you are 'green' and new to clean living or a seasoned veteran, *Living with a Green Heart* is filled with extraordinary tips and expert advice to help you along your green journey!"

—Dr. Alexis Daniels, D.C., CACCP, Daniels Center for Vitality at Sports Academy

"Gay is one of the foremothers of the environmental movement. She helped create a new breed of activist. She recognized early that in addition to business and political will, we need people to vote with their dollars. With plenty of historical references, Gay provides myriad ways to make a positive personal impact."

—Zem Joaquin, founder, ecofabulous and Near Future Summit,
co-creator, Cradle to Cradle Product Innovation Institute

"Get ready to enjoy having a fantastic tour guide as you embark on your own "green journey" alongside Gay Browne. Her practical style and approach will inspire and lead you to make lots of small changes in your life that will build habits—and habits will last a lifetime! Her goal is to help you lead a happier, healthier, and more grateful lifestyle!"

—Dave Aardsma, Founder at Aardsma Environmental Solutions Inc.

"The last fifty years have seen this planet become saturated with toxins from plastics, pesticides, personal care products, and industrial manufacturing. To prevent these environmental pollutants and toxins from affecting you, your family, and your child, the first step is awareness and knowledge, the second step is reducing exposure and prevention. Take this extremely well crafted book into your home and let it guide you through everything you need to know, to clean and create a healthy home and personal environment, for you and your family."

—Murray Clarke, President, Childlife Essentials

"Gay Browne is an Earth Angel. *Living with a Green Heart* is for those dreamers that want to 'wake up' and take practical steps towards a better world today."

—Ryland Engelhart, Owner, Cafe Gratitude and Gracias Madre, co-founder of Kiss the Ground

"In this comprehensive and engaging book, Gay Browne shows us how to look at the world through a green lens, revealing the myriad hazards and challenges of our everyday environment, and explains how, by focusing our attention and taking action, we can live significantly healthier lives. Whether it's the air you breathe, the water you drink, or the products you use, Gay offers sensible, practical solutions for safely navigating the countless chemical pitfalls that constantly confront us."

—Laurie Benenson, film producer

"We all want to protect our beautiful planet. We've cut back on water use and gotten rid of plastic bottles. But there's so much more we can do, and this book shows us how. It takes a passionate, committed agent of change like Gay Browne to guide us toward living green."

—Cecilia Peck, Documentary Filmmaker

"If we are ever going to save our planet, each individual has to begin to understand their role in the health of the planet and effect on their immediate environment. In *Living with a Green Heart*, Gay Browne clearly lays out our individual responsibilities with examples from daily life. If you care about our planet, this book shines a bright light into our collective futures."

—Evan Rofheart, Divine Energy Healer

"The planet needs a 'Green Heart,' and this book is an overflowing of Gay Browne's 'Green Heart.'"

—Sadhguru

LIVING WITH A GREEN HEART

*How to Keep Your Body, Your Home, and
the Planet Healthy in a Toxic World*

GAY BROWNE

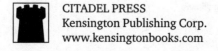

CITADEL PRESS
Kensington Publishing Corp.
www.kensingtonbooks.com

CITADEL PRESS BOOKS are published by

Kensington Publishing Corp.
119 West 40th Street
New York, NY 10018

PUBLISHER'S NOTE
The reader is advised that this book is not intended to be a substitute for an assessment by, and/or advice from, an appropriate medical professional(s). This book contains general information regarding health and should be viewed as purely educational in nature.

The author has made diligent efforts to include Internet addresses that are accurate at the time of publication, however neither the author nor the publisher is responsible for inaccurate or incomplete addresses, or for changes occurring after this book was printed and published. Moreover, the publisher and the author have no control over any such third-party Internet sites or the content contained thereon, and are not responsible for any such content.

All Kensington titles, imprints, and distributed lines are available at special quantity discounts for bulk purchases for sales promotions, premiums, fund-raising, educational, or institutional use. Special book excerpts or customized printings can also be created to fit specific needs. For details, write or phone the office of the Kensington sales manager: Kensington Publishing Corp., 119 West 40th Street, New York, NY 10018, attn: Sales Department; phone 1-800-221-2647.

CITADEL PRESS and the Citadel logo are Reg. U.S. Pat. & TM Off.

ISBN-13: 978-0-8065-3900-3
ISBN-10: 0-8065-3900-3

First trade paperback printing: April 2019

10 9 8 7 6 5 4 3 2

Printed in the United States of America

Library of Congress CIP data is available.

Electronic edition: April 2019

ISBN-13: 978-0-8065-3901-0
ISBN-10: 0-8065-3901-1

*This book is dedicated to Alex, Colin, and Katie
who with their unconditional love, taught me
how to live with a green heart.*

CONTENTS

FOREWORD

By Terry Tamminen

Who hasn't found peace and inspiration walking through a forest, diving into ocean waves, or experiencing the simple pleasures of a park filled with songbirds? We need no PhD to tell us that these are more enriching moments in life than countless hours sitting at a desk or trapped in a car on a busy freeway. Yet many studies have indeed made the clear connection between nature and human health. In addition to lowering blood pressure and improving memory function, spending time outdoors is a proven stress reliever.

Knowing this, we have tried to make our homes more like the forest, filling them with potted plants or maintaining backyard gardens. We condition the air to make it more like taking a breath on a mountain top. We filter water to give it qualities akin to a clear cold spring. But the sad truth is that just as we have degraded our natural surroundings with pollution, overconsumption, waste, and climate change, the environment in our homes and workplaces now contain the same stressors in the form of air pollution, toxic "cleaning" products, harmful pesticides in our foods, and lethal heavy metals in our drinking water. What was once a sanctuary for the human body, spirit and mind—an attempt to savor the benefits of nature in the midst of the dense urban jungle—has now become the very epicenter of self-destruction.

So what can we do about this? Demand action from our government? When I served as the secretary of the California Protection Agency, I saw firsthand the benefits of regulating the exposure to chemicals used in everyday life. But I also saw its limitations. There are literally hundreds of thousands of potentially harmful substances and compounds, with new ones added to commerce every day, and even well-meaning government officials simply can't keep pace. Moreover, what was once thought safe can no longer be trusted. For example, in 1946 regulators established exposure limits for benzene, one of the most toxic constituents of gasoline fumes, at 100 parts per million (ppm). Today we know that benzene exposure causes lung and other cancers, so the exposure limit has been reduced to 0.5 ppm, 200 times lower than was thought safe just three generations ago.

If government alone can't protect us, can we count on corporations to produce products that are always safe? Okay, such a foolish question hardly needs an answer as findings emerge revealing how the sugar industry lied to consumers for decades about the dangers of its products to human health, and how they then taught the "denial" tactics to tobacco companies and later to oil and coal companies that also faced regulation of their harmful products.

No, government and big business will not always put our well-being first. It's up to each of us to self-educate and take action. That's where this amazing book becomes an invaluable guide to the future.

In *Living with a Green Heart*, my good friend Gay Browne describes actions we can take that can simultaneously improve our well-being and repair our planet. Choices we can make in everyday lifestyle decisions that effectively have the power to spearhead a revolution redefining health and accessibility to "green" lives. Gay has considered everything from water quality to toothpaste in understanding that we all have the capacity to be part of the solution to the environmental challenges we face at home and around the globe. *Living with a Green Heart* is the embodiment of the old adage "think globally, but act locally."

People will always move faster than government or businesses. Our "leaders" will follow if we demand change, and consumer choices will influence corporate priorities, products, and accountability. The power lies within each of us to make decisions that protect us from the thousands of still unregulated chemicals and toxins remaining on the market, keep us from adding even more waste to a planet being chocked by plastic and pollutants, and help us materially change the world and the places where we live and work. Our actions, empowered by great books like this one, will make all the difference in the quest to create a society that develops and exercises its "green heart."

Shakespeare said, "Nature's bequest gives nothing, but doth lend . . . / Then how when Nature calls thee to be gone, / What acceptable audit canst thou leave?" Giving room for your green heart to flourish, and helping others to do so, will leave a legacy that would inspire even Shakespeare to write sonnets of joy.

Terry Tamminen is CEO of the Leonardo DiCaprio Foundation. An author and activist, he is former secretary of the California EPA.

INTRODUCTION:

My Green Story

I was not born an environmentalist. I was, however, raised during the great social unrest of the sixties, listening to the rebellious ballads of Patti Smith and the love songs of the Beatles, and selling POW bracelets as a student in junior high. I knew I wanted to grow up and do my part in righting the injustices of society, but I didn't know until much later in life that fighting for environmental health would be how I would do it. The environmental movement in the United States was just beginning, and it hadn't yet reached my small Southern community. I thought green was homegrown marijuana.

I first became aware of how the environment and our personal habits and decisions can affect our health back in 1992. I broke out in hives and couldn't figure out why. I visited several doctors and was tested for everything from allergies and thyroid disease to diabetes and HIV. I had so many blood tests, I felt like a human pincushion! Then, my friend urged me to go see Murray Clarke, D.Hom., M.Hom., L.Ac, a homeopathic practitioner based in Santa Monica, California.

Murray changed my life. His approach was entirely different from that of my internist. As a homeopath, he believed in treating the cause rather than the symptom, and after getting an extensive medical history from me, during which he learned that I had just finished a dose of a medication to prevent malaria while on a trip to Indonesia, he determined that my hives were likely a result of my kidney and liver struggling to deal with and detoxify the drug. After a week of a homeopathic kidney and liver support regimen, my hives disappeared. From that day on, Murray became my primary health care practitioner as well as my friend.

Coincidently, at that time, the home I was living in with my soon-to-be husband Tony, was quite literally falling down around us and needed to be rebuilt. Murray suggested we take the opportunity to make our home environmentally friendly and take steps to control the indoor air quality. Since I am an asthmatic and the quality of the air is critical to my health, he recommended Mary Cordaro, a building consultant and certified baubiologist. I had no idea what baubiologie was, but I learned quickly that BauBiologie is the study of how living and work environments affect human health and living systems. Since 1989, Mary has been consulting to clients who want to live or work in healthy environments. Her clients are usually new or prospective parents who want their children to start out in a healthy environment, or those who suffer from allergies, asthma, or chemical and electrical sensitivities. She directs a team of experts to diagnose and solve indoor air quality problems in homes and offices. For remodels and new construction, she specifies "beyond green" healthy building and interior materials. Further research revealed that Mary was the best person for the job. Her guidance was invaluable. I learned so much, like why choosing the right plywood and formeldeyhde-free glues were critical to the future outgassing of your home, or how some granite and marble have higher levels of radiation than other materials, and the significance of waxing floors versus applying a standard polyurethane finish. But the most valuable lesson she taught me was that the home is the most important place to start when greening your life. This is because, according to the EPA, indoor air can be two to five times more toxic than outdoor air. And since we spend 90 percent of our time indoors, the home and office can be a major contributor of exposures to toxic contaminants that include mold, EMFs, and chemicals in household and building products. (www.epa .gov/report-environment/indoor-air-quality)

Your home is where you let down your hair, rest your head, refresh your soul, and feed your body, and it is also the place where you are the most vulnerable. Your home is your sanctuary from the toxins of the outside world, both literally and figuratively.

Working with Mary made me feel a bit like Alice in Wonderland, falling down the rabbit hole into a whole new world—a green one. I had already been trying to live a healthier life by shopping in health food stores, but most of my green efforts had centered around my personal food choices, not my living environment. It took more than two years of blood, sweat and tears (and enduring crazy remarks from family and friends) to rebuild that house in Pacific Palisades, but when we were done, I could confidently say that we were living in the healthiest, most environmentally friendly home in all of Los Angeles. Our home was even featured in the *Los Angeles Times*. This was pre-LEED certification (that is, Leadership in Energy and Environmental Design, created by the US Green Building Council), the most popular green building certification, now used worldwide.

Although eating organic/local food and living in an eco-friendly home felt like living a green life, my real advocacy work didn't really begin until years later. In 2005, I found myself enjoying lunch on the patio of Michael's Restaurant in Santa Monica, with Tony and John Adams, the co-founders of the Natural Resources Defense Council. I listened intently as John spoke passionately about climate change and the work he and his group were doing to combat it. This was just before Al Gore's film *An Inconvenient Truth* had debuted and climate change became a household word, but I was mesmerized as he told us horror stories of environmental and species extinction. Something inside me shifted that afternoon. I knew I had to be part of this movement. Writing a check for a donation would help in the short term, but it was not going to satisfy the long-term needs required to effect change. To save the planet, we needed to create a change in human behavior and make people aware that their daily habits affected not only them but also the planet. When I left lunch that day, I shook John's hand and promised that I would find a way to help. Although I had no idea how I was going to do this, I knew from my fifteen-year career in marketing and advertising that the most effective way of getting people to hear your message was to make it personal. I wanted to find a way to communicate what I had learned from Murray and Mary about environmental health and wellness—how my daily actions affected the health of the planet and how the health of the planet was affecting me and my family.

For most of us, climate change is an abstract, distant danger, simply because, in most cases, we can't see it. But the truth is that more and more chemicals are seeping into our daily life. Our water, food, and air supply have become tainted from rising pollution levels everywhere. We are unconsciously ingesting food that was produced in ways that were damaging to the soil and the air we breathe, and the water we drink continues to be contaminated with toxins that are harmful to our health. Most people (including me) don't always take the time to read the labels on the products they are purchasing to know what is inside of them (and to be honest, the labels aren't always all that forthcoming). It never ceases to amaze me that people can often spend days and months analyzing and interviewing investment managers to manage their retirement account, but don't take the extra time it takes to look more closely at labels for ingredients that could potentially cause cancer. If our focus is not keeping toxins out of our everyday lives, we won't be able to live long enough to enjoy retirement anyway. Why do people put their financial security above their personal health and wellness? Is the concept of our eroding environment so scary that it is easier to look the other way? Or is the thought of trying to figure everything out just so overwhelming that people are paralyzed? Have our lives become so frenetic that we are just whirling around answering texts and emails trying to survive the day and missing the real purpose of life?

Then one day, I was browsing through a Michelin Guide in preparation for an upcoming trip and a bright green light bulb went off. Could I create a research-based methodology that would screen businesses and rate them according to how eco-friendly they were to help people shop, live, and eat green in their community?

In August of 2005, I was able to take some money out of our retirement account to start Greenopia, a company that was dedicated to educating people on how to live a green life. My first hire was Ferris Kawar, who was the Community Program Manager at Sustainable Works. He had been working for a non-profit that is supported by the City of Santa Monica to teach businesses and consumers how to lead eco-friendly lives. Once we developed the criteria, with the help of local experts, I added five researchers. For the next six months, our team walked door-to-door in Los Angeles, armed with yellow legal notepads, writing down what good green practices local businesses were employing. We surveyed more than ten thousand businesses to find a core list of eight hundred to fit our criteria, which we organized into a green leaf rated city guide.

On April 22, 2006, I found myself standing on the Third Street Promenade in downtown Santa Monica at the Earth Day Festival with Tony, our three children, and Greenopia's small team. We were all wearing pea-green Patagonia shirts embroidered with our new Greenopia leaf logo and handing out the very first edition of *Greenopia Los Angeles: The Urban Dweller's Guide to Green Living*. I still remember how excited I was. I was no longer someone who was just concerned about our environmental health and making donations; I was doing something to make the world a better place. I was truly living with a green heart!

That first year we sold twenty thousand copies of the Los Angeles guide and then made the decision to expand to San Francisco in 2007 and New York City in 2008. By 2009, we did a revised Los Angeles edition and in total had sold 70,000 copies; published an online Santa Barbara edition, and had created a website, Greenopia.com and a mobile app that was getting nearly one million visitors a month. And now there's this book.

Every day the headlines are filled with stories of dangerous chemicals leaking into water supplies and lethal pesticides or huge amounts of antibiotics being allowed in food production. We're hearing more and more about global warming, and even though it has become a hot political topic, we're seeing greater evidence of it in our daily lives—from severe weather to decreased air quality and rising rates of asthma. Living in today's world is complicated and trying to make sense of competing health recommendations and environmental issues can be confusing. With all the green marketing and green washing (fake claims about what's green) today, sorting through what's environmentally friendly for the planet and what's good for our health is overwhelming. This book is designed to simplify this complicated subject and offer solutions in a way that fits within your budget and your busy lifestyle. To make your voice more powerful and fix our broken system, it is important to support efforts like Arlene Blum and the Green Science Policy Institute, who create and advocate for green chemistry on a global scale.

I would like to tell you that after reading this you will be able to live a 100 percent toxin-free life and the planet will be completely healed, but I can't. What I hope this book will do is to inspire you to become more conscious about the things you do in your daily life. If you make better-informed choices in your daily decisions—the food you eat, the water you drink, where you choose to live, the personal-care products you buy, the type of bedding you sleep on, and the clothing you wear—each little change will help make your life and the life of everyone on the planet a little healthier.

How Green Is Your Heart?

Before we jump into all the recommendations, you might want to take this test, as a way of creating your baseline. Answer each question and then tally up your answers. For every a) answer give yourself 1 point; b = 2 points; c = 3 points; and d = 4 points.

1. **Is there an air purification system in your home, office or school?**
   a) No, I don't see the point in purifying the air I breathe; it seems to be fine the way it is!
   b) No, but I have often thought about installing an air purification system in my home.
   c) Yes, I have an air purifier in my home, but not in my other daily environments.
   d) Yes, I'm lucky! My air is pure at home, work and/or school.

2. **How often do you purchase a plastic water bottle?**
   a) Every day—plastic water bottles are my main hydration source when I'm not home.
   b) Once or twice a week—plastic water bottles help me hydrate in a pinch!
   c) Every once in a while, when I forget to carry my personal water bottle . . . oops!
   d) Never—I couldn't live without reusable water bottle at my fingertips.

3. **How often is your cell phone close to your body?**
   a) Always, my phone is my other half. It's a part of me.

   b) Most of the time, but I turn it off/put it away at bedtime!

   c) Work in progress. I am away from my phone more than I used to be!

   d) My phone is not usually on my person, but kept in a purse/briefcase, etc.

4. Do you consider the ingredients in your shampoo and conditioner an important factor when choosing a product?

   a) No, the ingredients in my hair products aren't important to me; I just want my hair to look fabulous.

   b) Sometimes, but it's not very important to me

   c) Yes, but it's not the most important consideration for me when choosing a product.

   d) Yes, I always check my products on the Cosmetics Database before bringing them into my home. Better safe than sorry!

5. Do you think your skincare has an impact on the environment?

   a) Definitely not— if it does anything at all, it only affects my skin, right?

   b) Not really. If there's any environmental impact at all, it's probably small.

   c) To some extent; I try to buy products with fewer synthetic chemicals when I can.

   d) Yes, I love dolphins and I choose makeup that won't hurt our marine life when I wash it off at night.

6. How often do you to purchase organic food?

   a) Never—it's too much work and too expensive . . . and I bet it doesn't taste as good!

   b) Seldom. It's nice to buy organic when I can, but it's not essential.

c) Often. I usually try to buy organic at my local grocery store.

d) Always. It is very important to me that my produce, meat, and dairy are organic, and I buy from a local producer at a farmer's market whenever I can.

7. **If you eat meat, how often do you consume it?**

a) Every day! It's delicious!

b) Several times a week—meat is an important staple in my household.

c) About once a week—it's a nice treat

d) Never. The closest I get to a cow is an Impossible Burger!

8. **Do you think that the type of cleaning products you use have an impact on your health or the environment?**

a) No, I don't think chemicals in cleaning products really affect me or the environment.

b) Somewhat, I try to buy nontoxic products if I can .

c) Yes, I usually buy nontoxic products, but some of the toxic products just work better!

d) Yes of course! I can't feel good about cleaning if I'm polluting our environment while doing it!

9. **How often do you use a Teflon pan to cook with?**

a) Always. I don't want my eggs to stick!

b) Often—it makes my clean up easier.

c) Rarely—I prefer to use other types of cookware.

d) Cast iron all the way.

10. **Have you ever had your blood tested for heavy metals or other toxins?**

a) No, I didn't know that this test was available/important to my health.

b) I've thought about it, but I'm not sure how to get started with the process.

c) Once, and I learned a lot about my body!

d) Yes, I have my blood tested for heavy metals regularly.

11. **When making a clothing purchase, how often do you think about the materials used and the manufacturing process?**

   a) Never. It doesn't matter how my clothes are made, as long as they look good!

   b) Rarely. I don't usually pay attention to what my clothes are made of.

   c) Often. I prefer to buy sustainable clothing that is made of natural materials when I can.

   d) Always. I also buy less. Why buy clothes I don't absolutely love when they just sit in the back of my closet.

12. **How often do you print documents double-sided?**

   a) I've never printed double-sided, and I don't see why I should start now.

   b) Rarely. It can be annoying for whoever is going to read the document.

   c) Often, but some documents can't be printed double-sided.

   d) Always. It cuts down on paper usage in my office and I only print when necessary.

13. **When driving or purchasing a car, do you consider its environmental impact?**

   a) No, as long as I like my car, it doesn't matter to me how it affects the environment.

   b) I've thought about it, but I bet it's probably too expensive.

   c) No, but the next car I buy will be an electric or a hybrid.

   d) Yes, of course! The next car I buy will be an electric! But why drive? I take public transportation, bike or walk whenever I can!

14. **When making a purchase, do you consider a company's sustainability policy?**
    a) No, what a company chooses to do is their responsibility; my consumer choices make no difference
    b) Sometimes, but I'm not necessarily aware of this information when shopping, so it's difficult.
    c) Yes, I prefer to support sustainable companies when possible.
    d) Yes, always. I know that as a consumer, my purchase is my support for that company's policies.

15. **How often do you donate time or resources to environmental organizations on either a local or global scale?**
    a) Never. I don't think my participation really makes a difference.
    b) Every once in a while; I love the polar bears, but my life is already hectic and its not a priority.
    c) Often. When I have time, I enjoy supporting our planet.
    d) Regularly—it is important to me to be involved in affecting local and/or global change.

LEVELS OF "GREEN GROWTH"

1. (15–25) **SEED**—You're ready to start growing toward a greener life (just add a little filtered water and some unprocessed plant food). Get a houseplant and watch it grow.

2. (26–37) **SAPLING**—You've already started down the path toward a greener future (just need a little more nurturing and knowledge). Plant a tree to celebrate with One Tree Planted (reforest the Amazon or help California recover from the wildfires).

3. (38–49) **EVERGREEN**—You've already developed a solid knowledge base and some good habits (keep pushing and growing upwards). Pick one environmental habit you would like to strengthen (sustainable shopping, planting, advocacy), and spend the next 30 days growing in this area. Ask a friend to track your progress.

4. (50–60) **REDWOOD**—Congrats! You have a wealth of knowledge that you use for the good of the earth (there's always more to learn, never stop growing and reaching). Get one friend to help you on your journey to make the world better one step at a time.

Health Check

We live in a stressful world. We have job stress, family stress, health stress, and emotional stress, but the stress that no one talks about and the one that intersects with all the others is what I call "Environmental Stress Syndrome," the next public health pandemic. Our bodies are under incredible environmental stress. There are 90,000 chemicals on the market today. Scientists have found hundreds of these chemicals in humans. A study spearheaded by The Environmental Working Group found 287 toxic chemicals in the blood of newborn babies. According to Dr. Alexis Daniels, D.C., pesticides and BPA are just a few of the many chemicals that weaken the four main barriers of protection our body has: gut, skin, lungs, and blood-brain. Unrelenting chemical or environmental insults degrade these barriers leaving our immune systems susceptible to anything and everything in our environment. Furthermore, instead of regulating our own cells and fighting off foreign invaders like viruses and bacteria, our immune systems are in a constant state of attack—this inflammatory response becomes switched on, all day, every day.

It seems like common sense: If evidence exists that a chemical is causing harm, we should get it out of our lives. Simple changes can have a huge impact. A study out of UC Berkeley, The Hermosa Study, showed that when 100 teen girls switched to personal care products without chemicals such as phthalates, parabens, triclosan, and oxybenzone for three days, blood tests showed that levels of certain potent hormone disruptors had been reduced by 45 percent. Forty-five percent in three days! Small changes build habits. Habits will last you a lifetime. Pay attention to ingredients. Buy organic. Carry a reusable water bottle and refuse single-use plastic. These habits become part of who you are, so when you're confronted with a new choice, your new habits will guide you.

What's really problematic is the discrepancy of what is legally acceptable and what is actually safe. The EPA's standards have changed during various administrations, so what they consider "legal" may not be "safe" by scientific standards. Some consumers have a false sense of security that every product on the shelf is healthy and safe since we have these government agencies monitoring them, but sadly, that just isn't the case.

Environmental stress is the silent killer that lives with us day in and day out and the one we may not pay much attention to until the day someone we love tells us over lunch that they have been diagnosed with stage three lymphoma or lung cancer. Or we notice that the sun, which we used to love to worship, now hurts our skin because the ozone layer has gotten so thin. It could be that moment when you hear on the news that plastics now outnumber sea life six to one, and when the sun breaks down plastic trash that gets thrown into the ocean, the plastic forms tiny microbeads that the fish mistake for food—and that we then ingest when we eat seafood. That's when it hits you that it's time to take action to change things for yourself, your family, and the planet.

As I've said, I first discovered the connection between our environment and our health when I met Dr. Murray Clarke. His homeopathic treatment was nothing short of a miracle to me, and I became intrigued to learn what other ways homeopathy could heal. In particular, I wanted to know how it could help my son, who was having trouble in school.

My son, Alex, had normal scores on his Apgar test for newborn health at birth and had later hit all the medical milestones: nursing well, using his hands, facial recognition, sitting up, talking, and so on. But he had difficult reactions to immunizations and seemed to struggle with being around a lot of children and in his schoolwork. After a visit to Murray, we realized that there was a good chance that Alex had been exposed to significant amounts of mercury during gestation. When I was pregnant, I had a mouthful of silver amalgam fillings and I ate canned tuna fish almost every day because I was a working mom on a budget who craved salt. At the time, the dangers of high mercury levels in fish like tuna weren't widely known. Murray thought that the mercury load that Alex had been carrying might have been compounded by routine immunizations and possibly a contributor to his difficulty in learning. Although we will never know for sure, I worked closely with Murray and other health professionals to get Alex's system cleaned up, and I'm happy to say that Alex has gone on to graduate from college, earn an MBA and is working on a his second master's degree. He is a whiz-bang data and marketing expert, a gourmet chef, and flies his own Cessna 185.

It is important to note here than I am not telling anyone to not immunize their children. I am strongly recommending that you consider delaying immunizations to allow their little bodies to get stronger to be able to handle the immunization load. I immunized my children starting at two years of age and spread the vaccinations throughout their pre- and elementary school years. If this issue speaks to you, I highly recommend that you read the book by Robert F. Kennedy, Jr. called *Thimerosal: Let the Science Speak*.

I also want to say that not everyone has a problem with mercury; each of us processes, digests, absorbs and eliminates foods, chemicals, and heavy metals in our own individual way. Some people will have more difficulty than others with how their body can neutralize, detoxify, and eliminate mercury and other metals like lead, cadmium, arsenic, etc. What I do know is that before I got pregnant again, I chelated myself—a process which is used to get rid of unwanted metals from the body—and my next two children were born with normal or low amounts of mercury and other heavy metals and did not have any of the learning issues that my older son had experienced.

I do not believe in a one-size-fits-all approach to health. As you read this book, you will have the chance to make individual decisions of what will work for you. Here are some things I would recommend to move toward a greener, healthier life:

- Test yourself for heavy metals and other toxins like pesticides or plastic. You can do this through a simple blood panel test with your doctor or yourself, by sending in a swatch of your hair and having it analyzed by Doctor's Data or The Great Plains Laboratory. Also, The Silent Spring Institute has a "DeTox Me Action Kit" that can detect the presence of the ten most common household chemicals that can accumulate in your body. If you find that you have toxins, talk to your doctor, or find one who knows the proper protocol for chelating and detoxifying. Chelating will help get rid of these unwanted metals but can also strip away the good ones, so if this is something you want to do, please do it under the supervision of a doctor or other practitioner who can keep a watchful eye over you as you go through this process.

- Ask your parents or siblings for a detailed family medical history so you can see what your genetic predispositions are, and ask your doctor if he or she has access to genetic blood testing. DNA plays a key role on how your body handles environmental stress. As Murray Clarke says, "from the field of epigenetics which studies the effect and impact of the environment on our inherited DNA, we now know for certain that at any point in time in any child's or adult's life, their current state of health is the sum result of the DNA they were both born with, how their immune system has developed since birth, and how and what their body and DNA has been exposed to in the environment. Epigenetic research now also shows that a person's exposure to metals like mercury will not only impact their current state of health but can also directly change their DNA genome, meaning that now the parents' DNA has been altered by their exposure to environmental toxins and this transformed and impaired DNA may then be passed on to their offspring. The science of epigenetics now fully places into perspective how this worldwide exposure to all sorts of man-made and industrial toxins and pollutants is not only affecting everyone's current state of health but is also changing the human genome and compromising the integrity and health of the DNA of the next unborn generation."
- Find a biological dentist, and if you still have silver amalgam fillings, ask to have them removed correctly and safely and replaced with composite or ceramic fillings. You want someone who knows the proper protocol for this so that the mercury doesn't leak into your bloodstream by accident.
- Review the stressors in your life, and see how you can lessen or eliminate them. This might mean saying goodbye

Some of the Choices Available

When I started my health journey with Murray, I became fascinated by the different healthcare approaches that focused on the causes, not the symptoms, of a disease. Below is a list of the different types of healthcare practices so that you can decide which one (or ones) may be right for you.

- **ACUPUNCTURE:** Insertion of needles to specific points on the body to unblock meridians and allow energy to circulate to specific vessels, tissues, organs, and glands and to remove blockages.
- **ALLOPATHIC (WESTERN) MEDICINE:** Treatment usually pharmaceutically based to address symptoms that arise in isolated parts of the body.
- **CHIROPRACTIC:** Physical adjustments of the body focused on the spine rather than the whole body, as with osteopathic medicine (see below), to remove obstructions in the spine and facilitate energy flow throughout the central nervous system.
- **FUNCTIONAL OR INTEGRATIVE MEDICINE:** Treats the whole person using all appropriate therapies. Over the last several years we have seen the terms of functional or integrative medicine being introduced into the medical lexicon. Medical doctors have begun to educate themselves on modalities and methods outside of the customary confines and limited pharmaceutical approaches of allopathic medicine. These doctors are now beginning to utilize and integrate these other modalities from the fields of naturopathic, nutritional medicine, acupuncture and herbal medicine and in this way are providing a more comprehensive and holistic diagnosis and treatment model.
- **HERBAL MEDICINE:** The use of plants to prevent, treat, and cure disease. There are three primary kinds of herbal medicine: Chinese (diagnoses the underlying condition based on symp-

continued on p. 18

continued from page 17

toms and observation of the tongue, pulse, and physical and emotional characteristics); Ayurvedic (diagnoses the condition based on symptoms, body measurements, diet suitability, digestive capacity, physical fitness, features, and age), and Western (diagnoses based on presenting physical symptoms and history). Practitioners will all prescribe an herbal formula based on their own methods.

- **HOLISTIC MEDICINE:** Often used as a catchall term for any alternative system of medicine, but in reality, it refers to certain approaches of medicine, such as physical, nutritional, emotional, spiritual, environmental, recognizing the whole individual's state of health.

- **HOLISTIC/BIOLOGICAL DENTISTRY:** Refers to the health of the mouth, which is intricately connected to the rest of the body and situated close to the brain. There are now a growing number of dentists who understand the intimate connection between oral health and overall health and the importance of not placing any toxic materials or metals into the teeth and mouth cavity.

- **HOMEOPATHIC MEDICINE:** Centers on the comprehensive view of the individual that uses a holistic approach, based on German physician Samuel Hahnemann's doctrine of like cures like.

- **NATUROPATHIC MEDICINE:** The approach of wellness through diet, nutrition, exercise, herbal medicine, and homeopathy.

- **NUTRITIONAL MEDICINE:** Evaluation of the nutritional status of the individual through urine, blood, stool, and hair analysis.

- **OSTEOPATHIC MEDICINE:** Specializes in adjusting and manipulating both the body and the brain to correct imbalances, poor alignment, or obstructions that interfere with the normal flow of energy, fluids, and nourishment through your brain, nervous system, immune system, lymphatic system, and body.

to those people around you whose toxic behavior might be affecting you more than you care to admit.

Staying in good health is the most sustainable thing any of us can ever do. Without good health we can't do anything. Taking care of yourself and your family is the best way to protect your future and the future of the planet. A healthy life is a happy life. As you will read in the pages to come, living with a green heart is about finding simple ways (and bigger ways if you choose) to lessen the effects of environmental stress syndrome in your own life and at the same time, collectively help the greater good of the planet.

Getting Started

I choose to live my life with a green heart.

As you read through the pages of this book, one thing you may notice is that each section starts with an intention. As Jill Willard, my friend and author of *Intuitive Being* says, words are powerful. One of the best ways to make a change is to create an intention. She explains that only in doing so, can you become captain of your own ship. Jill and I both believe setting an intention is the first step towards living with a green heart. Without intention, I would not be writing these words.

My meeting with John Adams and watching *An Inconvenient Truth* were watershed events that led me to set the intention that I wanted to be part of the solution instead of contributing to the problem. This passion led me to environmental restoration groups like Waterkeeper Alliance, Conservation International, The Nature Conservancy, Earth Justice, Kiss the Ground, Tree People, Friends of the Earth and the Environmental Working Group (EWG), among others. My original intention of raising money to help these NGOs save our planet shifted dramatically when I realized that no amount of money could save the world; we all needed to take an active part. It was after my lunch with John that I dreamed up the idea for Greenopia, a research-based green city directory that would guide people toward businesses that could help them live, shop, and eat green. Now over ten years later, I am more committed than ever to educating people on the avalanche of toxins in our daily world and finding healthy ways to deal with the effects of climate change on our society and psyche. I am writing this book with the intention of lessening your environmental stress by breaking down this complex issue in a practical way, and offering simple solutions that each one of us can take on a daily basis to improve our own health and the health of the planet.

We share a collective intention. Like me, you've made a conscious choice to live with a green heart. But in order to effect real change, you'll need to get more specific than that. You are steering your own ship, and you will decide what choices you will make to live every day with the green intentions that work best for you, your family, and your life circumstances.

You may read this book with the mindset of greening a particular area of your home or with specific health concerns or allergies that require you to be more knowledgeable of toxic ingredients and alternative choices. Your intention may solely be to help the planet. You may read it cover to cover or skip to the sections you are most interested in.

This is not a one-size-fits-all approach. It's up to each of you to decide what area calls you the most, where you can affect the most change, and what you can fit into your lifestyle and your budget.

To properly set an intention, I recommend that you do two things to start. First, write it down. Studies have shown that when people write down intentions and goals they are more likely to achieve them. The second thing you should do is post your intention in a place where you will see it every day. If you're visual, as I am, creating a vision board illustrating your overall intentions is also a great idea. I keep this vision board in my closet, so I see it every time I get dressed.

My initial intention led to a green ripple effect in my life and to me becoming an environmental health advocate. Your intention may take you elsewhere. The one thing I am certain of is that intentions affect change, and one green intention leads to another and another and collectively to a more environmentally healthy planet.

I know that as you read through this book, it may all seem to be so overwhelming that you might want to put your head down and do nothing at all. But as I told my children when I was teaching them to ride their bikes, don't look down, look where you're going. As His Royal Highness Prince Charles says so well in his book *Harmony: A New Way Of Looking At Our World*, the planet has fallen out of harmony with the natural rhythm of life and we can no longer separate what we are from what we do. We are at a tipping point on this planet where ignoring environmental stress is no longer an option. I don't expect that everyone who reads this book will take every green heart action I suggest. Everyone has different needs and means. However, I do encourage you to develop a personalized approach to your own environmental health and take it to heart. Here are my own personal ground rules for living with a green heart.

Be Open-Minded

The environment has become a controversial issue. There are those who deny climate change and those who like to believe that the organic label on a pint of raspberries is just a way to make more money. I am not one of them, and I will guess that if you went so far as to purchase this book, neither are you. But reading this book might push you out of your comfort zone so I will ask you to approach what you read with an open mind and try experimenting with new brands and new ways of doing things. Sometimes when deciding whether or not to buy organics, the added expense will cause you to wrestle with what is healthy and what fits your budget. You are the only one who can make these decisions, but just knowing your options is a step in the right direction.

Be Compassionate

Kermit the Frog is right; it isn't always easy being green. Nor is there only one way to do it. As you start to make changes, be kind to yourself. It's impossible to live 100 percent with a green heart every hour of every day. Forgiving yourself is a more loving approach than judging yourself on what you are not changing. Celebrate the small changes you are making and remember it is not just your health you are improving, but the health of the planet as well.

Be Educated

If you get nothing else out of this book, I hope you make reading labels a daily practice. You will learn a lot of terminology that is used in packaging and is designed to get you to buy something, not necessarily because it is good for you. Maintain a healthy dose of skepticism when reading, as labeling can often be misleading. Asking questions is the best way to get answers to things that are important to you. If you can't pronounce it, chances are you don't want to ingest it or put it on your skin.

Be a Conscious Consumer

We'll talk a lot in the book about companies that are increasingly committed to operating in sustainable and ethical manners. Support those companies. The more demand there is for products made with fewer toxins and with more responsible methods, the more other companies will follow suit. That's good for us personally and for the greater green good. Where you spend your money is the most powerful way of effecting change.

Be Practical

We all live on a budget. Some of the changes I suggest implementing may be outside of yours. Respect that. Not everyone can afford to install an air-filtration system, but most of us can afford a green houseplant that will also improve our indoor air quality. What's most important is to honor that you are taking steps, however big or small, to help save our planet.

Be Respectful

Living with a green heart means being respectful of your body, your health, your community, and the planet, and giving them the care, attention, and love they deserve. Hold everyone in high esteem, even those who aren't on the green path with you. They especially need more love. Don't judge others if they don't share your sustainable point of view. Let them find their own way. Be helpful if they ask, but the best way to teach is by example.

Be Hopeful

Know that however dire things may sound or look, if you are willing to live with a green heart, one small green heart action taken each day will make a positive impact toward personal and environmental healing. As more of us are willing to jump on the green bandwagon, the greater our collective impact will be. To echo the famous words of Gandhi, "Be the change you want to see in the world."

Be Passionate

Greenopia's original mission has pivoted beyond eco-friendly businesses to include access to information that encompasses every aspect of living an environmentally safe life. Our original logo was a green leaf, but it has now been replaced with a green heart. The kind of change needed to improve our environmental health and heal the planet starts with an open heart. My hope is that the passion I have for living my life with a green heart will inspire you to lead your life that way too.

THE ELEMENTS:
Air, Water, and EMFs

I choose to breathe healthy air, drink clean water, and spend time away from my devices every day.

EVERY LIVING HUMAN BEING and animal on the planet needs air, water, food, and shelter to survive. The quality of and access to all of these requirements for life will decide how long and in what condition we will live. These shared elements are part of what's called the global commons, the Earth's shared natural resources. These resources have been heavily taxed over the past century due to industrial innovation and a growth in population. For all of us to survive and thrive on the planet, it is critical that we stop thinking just about ourselves and think about the others in our community, and how we can better share these resources without further depleting them to the point of exhaustion. Living this way requires us to raise our level of consciousness and develop the self-discipline to act less selfishly. Without slowing our consumption way down, the quality of life as we know it will drastically change.

The Air That You Breathe

I choose to inhale and exhale clean air.

I have always suffered with asthma. As a child, my asthma attacks terrified me. I can remember being cradled in the arms of my parents all night long, each of them taking turns sitting in the rocking chair as they tried to calm me, encouraging me to take sips of water because they had given me all the asthma medication I was allowed for the day. What sticks in my memory most, beyond the terror of not being able to breathe, was the feeling of being loved unconditionally by my parents, how much I hated having asthma, and how I wanted to kill whatever was causing the attacks so I could go on with my life.

Asthma continues to be an unwelcome intruder in my life—as it is in the lives of twenty-five million Americans. Dust, mold, freshly cut grass, certain types of pollen, and cold or flu season can trigger it, as can a perfume or heavily polluted air. I can't get rid of my asthma, but I do my best to control both the indoor and outdoor air that I breathe. This means avoiding prolonged exposure to environmental allergens whenever possible and taking the steps that I will outline in this section.

You don't have to have asthma to suffer the effects of poor air quality. Asthma is just one of many afflictions that are caused or exacerbated by unsafe and poor-quality air.

Air quality rose to public awareness in 1952, when London suffered through what came to be known as the "Great Smog." Fog combined with sulfurous fumes from coal fires, exhaust from vehicles, and smoke from power plants blanketed the city for five days. It is now considered the worst pollution crisis in European history, and it is estimated that it was responsible for the deaths of eight thousand to twelve thousand people. This disaster prompted Parliament to pass the Clean Air Act in 1956, and the city began its transition from coal for heat to gas, oil, and electricity. However, this was hardly enough to solve a global problem that over the years has been exacerbated by industrial society. In 1955, the United States established its own Clean Air Act, a law that was designed to control air pollution on a federal level, administered by the EPA. It was amended in 1965 by the Motor Vehicle Air Pollution Control Act, which authorized the federal government to set standards for controlling emission of pollutants from cars beginning with cars manufactured in 1968. This act is still in place and has since been amended in the 1990s to include air pollution from other toxic air pollutants. The State of California has its own pledge, the Climate Air Scoping Plan, that will reduce statewide emissions 40 percent below 1990 levels by 2030.

According to the Lancet Commission on pollution and health, pollution is the largest environmental cause of disease and premature death in the world today. Diseases caused by pollution were responsible for an estimated 9 million premature deaths in 2015—16 percent of all deaths worldwide—three times more deaths than from AIDS, tuberculosis, and malaria combined and 15 times more than from all wars and other forms of violence. In 2017, Boston University School of Public Health found that those who live within 1,500 feet of a highway have a greater likelihood of developing cardiovascular disease than those living twice as far away. According to the EPA, more than forty-five million Americans live within nine hundred feet of a major road, railroad, or airport. In their 2017 State of the Air report, the American Lung Association stated that despite progress, four in ten Americans are at risk of serious health effects from air pollution. Short-term health risks include irritated eyes, noses and throats, headaches, dizziness, and fatigue; long-term health risks include respiratory ailments, heart diseases, and cancer from particulate matter and gaseous pollutants.

Air pollution is made up of various quantities of substances. Particulate matter includes dust, smoke, pollen, tobacco smoke, animal dander, dust mites, molds, bacteria, and viruses. Gaseous pollutants are a result of the combustion process and come from sources including gas cooking stoves, vehicle exhaust, tobacco smoke, adhesives, paints, varnishes, cleaning products, and pesticides.

Outdoor air pollution is visible; you can see the smog and know it exists. However, indoor air pollutants are mostly invisible. Professors John Spengler, Joe Allen, along with Skye Flanigan at the Harvard T. H. Chan School of Public Health, have done an amazing job in researching the health effects of environmental pollution on indoor air. And while our highly industrialized society makes it challenging to control the quality of our outdoor air, there is much we can do to improve the air that we breathe indoors.

When I rebuilt our home in Pacific Palisades, my goal was to build a house free of toxins. With the help of Mary Cordaro and our contractor, Chet Hoover, we sourced formeldehyde-free plywood , used cotton insulation instead of fiberglass, eliminated varnishes on wood or any other surfaces, sealed air ducts, put filters on air conditioners and heaters, and used a state-of-the-art air purification system. But you don't have to completely rebuild your home to improve the

No More Toxic Dust

- Vacuum frequently and use a vacuum fitted with a high-efficiency particulate air (HEPA and carbon) filter.
- Wet mop uncarpeted floors.
- Microfiber cloths are best to wipe furniture as their smaller fibers cling to the dust and dirt particles.
- Caulk and seal cracks and crevices with low- to no-VOC materials to keep dust from accumulating.
- Use genuine HEPA and carbon filters on your air heating and cooling systems. Be mindful of loose terms such as "HEPA-grade" or "HEPA style."
- Electronic equipment is a source of chemical fire retardants and dust. Keep these devices clean.
- Increase ventilation.

quality of the air you breathe. There are lots of little steps that could have a significant impact.

Filtering Out Those Nasty Particulates

The dirty secret of outdoor air pollution is that outdoor air is brought into our buildings and the majority of our exposure to air pollution actually occurs within our homes and buildings. You may be surprised to learn that, according to the EPA, our indoor environment is two to five times more toxic than the outdoors. While that figure is startling, in a way it's good news because you have more control over the air you breathe indoors. Keeping your home clean, well ventilated, and free of dust particles is a good start. You also want to use an air cleaning filter.

There are two types of air cleaning devices for indoor use. If you have access to the source of the air supply in your home or workplace, the best way is to install an overall filtration system in the heating and air conditioning units. However, if this is not possible, the easiest way is to buy a portable HEPA and carbon filter. HEPA stands for "high-efficiency particulate air," which is a fancy way of saying that the filter works to capture particulates like dust mites and smoke and pull them out of the air. A certified HEPA or carbon filter will remove at least 99.97 percent of particles 0.3 microns or larger in diameter.

There are many portable HEPA and carbon filter options that you can move from room to room and range in price from $50 to more than $1,000. It is important to check in with *Consumer Reports* or the EPA website for up-to-date information on the best brands. Also, look at the filter's MERV (Minimum Efficiency Reporting Value), which can be found in the label or in the product description. The MERV rating

Beyond the HEPA Filter

- Mechanical filters capture particles on a filter material. Electronic air cleaners use electrostatic attraction. HEPA filters are in the mechanical category.
- Gas-phase and activated-carbon air filters remove gases and odors with a material called a sorbent.
- Ultraviolet germicidal irradiation cleaners and photocatalytic oxidation cleaners destroy all air pollutants using ultraviolet light technology.
- Awair smart-sensing devices monitor the quality of your air, displaying levels of temperature, humidity, CO_2, chemicals, and fine dust in your home and give recommendations for improvements.

should be an eleven or higher to safely remove unwanted particulates. Some filters use electrostatic precipitators or ionizer technology, which may make the problem worse by producing ozone—a lung irritant. If you have an air purifier of any sort, please make sure that you clean or change the filter on it at the recommended intervals. Also make sure the filter is the right size for the space it will be used in; what's suitable for a 150 square-foot bedroom might not be best for a 350 square-foot great room. There are HEPA and carbon filters in every budget, and they can be found in places like Bed, Bath & Beyond as well as Costco. My favorite brand is Rabbit Air.

Houseplants Help

A plant added to your living room decor not only looks pretty, it can also increase the humidity and decrease the levels of carbon monoxide and carbon dioxide (CO_2) in the air. Scientists at NASA, Pennsylvania State University, and the University of Georgia found that common houseplants can absorb a long list of volatile organic compounds (VOCs) through their leaves and roots, including benzene found in plastics, fabrics, and pesticides and formaldehyde-releasing preservatives found in some cosmetics and dish detergents. We will discuss preservatives in cleaning products more in depth later on. The plants that were the most effective include Japanese royal ferns, spider plants, Boston ferns, purple waffle plants, English ivy, areca palms, golden pothos, aloe vera, snake plants, and peace lilies. Plants are natural filters and have the added benefit of looking beautiful, so preserving those outside your home and bringing more into your home are great ways of ensuring good air filtration. It is important to note that any of these benefits will be negated if the plant is overwatered; overwatered plants cause mold. Also, often what is most effective in houseplants removing chemicals isn't necessarily the plant itself, but what it is potted in, such as activated charcoal.

Take the Bus or Train

To help cut down on the outside pollutants, when possible take public transportation, carpool, and take advantage of new shared riding services such as Zip Car. This sounds small, but by using less energy and fuel you are helping to reduce greenhouse gas emissions. Public transportation is the most cost-effective, energy-efficient thing you can do, other than walking or riding a bike. It's also a good way to feel a part of the larger human whole.

Plant a Tree

It's not just houseplants that help improve air quality. Trees do too! They absorb potentially harmful gases, including carbon dioxide, carbon monoxide, and sulfur dioxide. It has been reported that residential proximity to vegetation is associated with lower levels of stress, aggression, diabetes, stroke, and cardiovascular disease. Studies have shown that children living in greener areas have lower levels of asthma, blood pressure, and insulin resistance.

Trees Cleaning the Air

According to One Tree Planted, a global reforestation group based in Vermont, when you plant trees you are directly cleaning the air. As a tree matures, it can consume forty-eight pounds of CO_2 per year as it turns that CO_2 into parts of itself. It also releases enough oxygen to supply your needs for two years. These two effects help to give the Earth a healthier climate.

Green Heart Heroes

Since 1973, Andy Lipkis has been educating, inspiring, and engaging people to plant and care for trees in the Los Angeles area through the organization he founded called Tree People. He and his team, along with volunteers and more than two million students, have planted more than two million trees, which has dramatically impacted the watershed and the quality of life in Los Angeles. Andy believes more trees strategically planted in cities is the key to protecting personal and community health and safety, and creating great social and economic benefits. Andy and Tree People have shown that an "urban forest" is the fastest way to make cities resilient and protected from the rapidly increasing heat, fires, flooding, pollution, and water shortages caused by climate change.

Aruni Bhatnagar, Ph.D., is the Smith and Lucille Gibson Professor of Medicine at the University of Louisville, the director of the univer-

---

Trees and their canopies are not only linked to better air quality but also have been proven to reduce violence. A 10 percent increase in tree canopy area is associated with a 12 percent decrease in crime. So, the next time you want to breathe better and feel safer, stand under a tree or, better yet, go plant one. Picnicking under trees with a friend is one of my favorite ways to dine.

Pay a Visit to Mother Nature

The best way to breathe clean air is still to go out into nature. Every day, Mother Nature brings out the sun, grows new trees and plants, and delivers clean fresh air for the world. A walk in the park, a hike in the mountains, or just finding a tree to sit next to not only helps improve

sity's Diabetes and Obesity Center, a senior member of the Institute of Molecular Cardiology, and the codirector of the American Heart Association Tobacco Research and Addiction Center. He started the Institute for Healthy Air, Water, and Soil at the University of Louisville and created the new field of environmental cardiology. He and his team study how pollution affects the heart and blood vessels and how exposure to polluted air affects the risk of obesity and diabetes. His research is supported by several grants from the National Institutes of Health. In 2017, with the support of Christy Brown, a big-hearted and generous philanthropist from Louisville who shared Aruni's passion for creating a cleaner environment, he joined with The Nature Conservancy to create a program in the city of Louisville, Kentucky, called the Green Hearts Project to study the effect of trees in improving air quality, as a direct way to improve the quality of the city's air.

the quality of the air you take in, it has also been shown to improve your overall well-being by relieving stress, sharpening your thinking, and boosting your memory. "Forest bathing," a popular activity started in Japan, is now gaining in popularity all over the world. Forest bathing is not about getting naked and running through the woods, but it is about going out into nature, taking off your shoes, and putting your feet in water to alleviate the stress of our daily lives and get closer to nature.

Check the Air Quality in Your Area

I didn't pay much attention to daily air quality levels until I moved to Los Angeles in 1983, at the height of the city's smog problems. At that time, reporting on the PM2.5—a metric that measures atmospheric particulate matter that has a diameter of less than 2.5 microns—was something every network news anchor and disc jockey included in their daily broadcasts. This number was important because it meant that a particulate was so small and light there was a greater chance of inhaling it. For me, it meant never leaving home without my inhaler and avoiding being outdoors on poor air quality days. The air quality was so poor that despite having built a green home, I eventually ended up moving to Santa Barbara because my airflow was steadily decreasing at the rate of 5 percent a year. After twenty years, that was a significant loss and one that might have had me hooked up to a oxygen tank by the time I was sixty.

To check air quality levels in your area, look up the most recent American Lung Association State of the Air report at www.lung.org/our-initiatives/healthy-air/sota. Two good apps are Breezeometer and Purple Air, which is becoming a popular outdoor air quality measuring device.

Green Heart Actions

- Install a HEPA or carbon filter in your home and office.
- Purchase safer products—including building materials, cleaning supplies, and personal care products.
- Add more plants to your indoor environments and make sure to water them properly.
- Plant more trees: check with community organizations like Tree People and The Nature Conservancy to help you get started.
- Conserve energy by carpooling and using mass transit.
- Avoid exercising on high pollution days or in areas with high levels of air pollution, such as near busy roadways.

Water Is Life

I choose to drink clean water.

Every July from ninth grade through my sophomore year in college, I traveled north from Kentucky to the Boundary Waters where Ontario straddles the Minnesota border for a canoe trip. My companions were a group of kids led by my high school history teacher, Tom Grunwald. Waking up in Minnesota to the sun filtering through the tall pine trees and the smell of clean, sweet air after driving all night in a van was a welcome escape into the magic of the outdoors. As someone who's always suffered from asthma, these trips were nature's medicine for me.

What sticks in my memories the most is the water. Strapping on our backpacks and loading into our canoes and then pushing off into the Finger Lake of the Boundary Waters was like slipping into a new life. Each time we did it, I was able to wash away all the conflicts of home as I dipped my wooden paddle into the smooth surface of a lake.

The region we canoed, known as the Quetico, was a spectacular, untouched patch of wilderness with breathtaking vistas and the most pristine waterways I'd ever seen. The lakes were so clear and clean that we were able to take out our tin cups and drink the water from any place on a lake. The water was so pure, like nothing I had ever tasted before!

One summer in the late 1970s, the forest ranger told us that there were troubles in the water. Pollutants were floating around the edge of the lake, and the fish population had decreased. He explained that wastes from chemical plants had made their way into rivers and streams and that flushing unused medications down the toilets had resulted in low levels of antibiotics, hormones, and steroids polluting the water and harming fish. This news incensed us all. Our fresh, clean drinking water was being polluted! Instead of having the freedom to drink water from wherever we wanted on the lake, we were told we had to gather it from the center of the lake, where it was "generally safer."

I was heartbroken. But like most childhood heartbreaks, I pushed it to the recesses of my heart and mind. It wasn't until that lunch with John Adams three decades later that it resurfaced. As I listened to John describe the state of the water and the Earth, I suddenly realized that living and working in cities in my twenties and thirties had made me lose sight of something that at one point had been so near and dear to my life: nature and water.

I told John that water was something I had always felt was sacred and that I wanted to do something to help the clean water movement. He directed me to Steve Fleischi, then director of Heal the Bay in Santa Monica, and I signed up to be an active donor. It was through Steve that I heard the compelling Robert F. Kennedy Jr. speech for the first time. Kennedy had cofounded Hudson Riverkeeper, now known as Waterkeeper Alliance, after he discovered the fish of the

Hudson River were too polluted to eat. His passion and determination to reverse the damage we are doing to our water and fish was contagious and reaffirmed that I was finally on my path. Bobby had me hooked.

The Clean Water Act was passed in 1972 with the primary objective of restoring and maintaining the integrity of our nation's waters. Its primary purpose was to eliminate the discharge of pollutants into public waters so that water quality levels would be swimmable and fishable. This law was followed by the Safe Drinking Water Act (SDWA) in 1974, amended in 1986 and 1996, when the EPA decided to create standards for safe drinking water for national, state, and city public water systems. It is interesting to note that there are ninety-six chemicals with legally-enforceable Maximum Contamination Levels (MCLs) set by the SDWA, but there are hundreds of toxic chemicals in our water supply that are unregulated. Of the ninety-six MCLs, many fall short of protecting human health.

In 1993, Erin Brockovich woke up a lot of people when she sued the Pacific Gas and Electric Company for dumping approximately 370 million gallons of chromium-6–tainted wastewater into ponds around Hinkley, California, resulting in contaminated groundwater that scientists have linked with cancer. While she won that suit in a $333 million settlement, it was not enough to address the prob-

---

Chemicals That May Be Lurking In Your Water

Some of the chemicals that might be in your water supply are: arsenic, bacteria, chlorine, chloramines, fluoride, gasoline, hydrogen sulfate and sulfide, iron, iron bacteria, magnesium, high levels of nitrate, pesticides in herbicides, and radon.

lem. A 2017 update to a study she did in 2016 in partnership with the EWG revealed that 250 million people in all fifty states were drinking tap water with unsafe levels of toxic chemicals, an increase from 218 million in the original report! (www.ewg.org/tapwater/state-of-american-drinking-water.php) I wish I could say our waters are as pristine as they were on those camping trips to the Boundary Waters, but they're not. When problems get this pervasive in our world we wonder if there is anything we can do to make a significant difference and, more importantly, how we are going to protect ourselves and our families to ensure that the water we drink and bathe in is safe.

Test Your Drinking Water

You can no longer assume that the tap water coming out of your faucet is safe.

A great place to start to learn about possible chemicals in your water is EWG's Tap Water Database, where you can type in your zip code and search to find the contaminants found in the drinking water in your area. To find the state-certified laboratory in your area, call the EPA's National Primary Drinking Water Regulations at the safe drinking water hotline at 1-800-426-4791 or visit www.epa.gov/dwlabcert/contact-information-certification-programs-and-certified-laboratories-drinking-water

Knowing whether or not your drinking water is safe is key to living with a green heart, and since water is a fluid resource, it is important to have your drinking water tested periodically to make sure there are no changes and no new contaminants have infected your supply. Contaminants often do not affect the color of your water, nor do they necessarily affect the taste. The only way to know what's going on in your water is to test it.

Get a Water Filtration System

Once you know what you are dealing with, you'll be able to make better decisions about what kind of water filter meets your needs and your budget. There are different filters for specific water filtration needs.

Until you know the quality of your water, the simplest and most affordable fix is to buy a pitcher with a water filtration system. The pitcher filtration system is fairly simple. You fill the pitcher from the tap and the water runs through a filter, making it cleaner. The upside to pour-through pitchers is that they are portable, but the downside is that their water-filtration capabilities are limited as to what they filter. If you get one, make sure you change the filter regularly. But if I had to choose a countertop option, I would choose a gravity water purification system, such as a Big Berkey or a ProPur Big. These filters remove everything from viruses and bacteria to chlorine and fluoride, but still leaves the good minerals.

The second option is to buy a temporary filtration mount that hooks up to your kitchen sink's water faucet using a carbon technology. Aquasana, Brita, Culligan, Dupont, and PUR make faucet filters certified to remove contaminants, such as asbestos, chlorine, lead, insecticides, and trihalmethanes.

The third option—more permanent and more expensive—is to install an under-the-sink water-filtration system. There are many systems out there, and they can range in price from hundreds to several thousands of dollars. Many will eliminate a wide variety of contaminants, such as chlorine and chloramine. Reverse osmosis filters offer the broadest filtration. They also remove the minerals from your water that make it "hard." This can be beneficial if you prefer soft water; however, it also removes good minerals, such as calcium. My personal favorites are Kangen and Perfect Water. My Kangen filters also balance alkaline levels of my water, which help lower the acid in my stomach. Because the quality of water my family and I drink

---

What You Need To Know About Chlorine

Avoid it! When used as a water treatment it combines with organic matter to create compounds called trihalomethanes, also known as disinfectant byproducts. The most common is chloroform, a known carcinogen. Other risks from trihalomethanes include increased risks of bladder, kidney, and rectal cancers, and an increased risk of asthma.

---

on a daily basis is of upmost importance to me, I am willing to make this a priority in our budgetary expenditures.

The last and most expensive option to consider is a point-of-entry filtration system. In this case, the system is placed on the main water line before it enters your plumbing system. These are generally more expensive than filtering water as you use it, but they take care of clean water not just for drinking but for all your water needs. If you can convince your landlord or company to do this for your water supply or can afford to do it yourself, it is the very best way to ensure that your overall quality of water is the best.

EWG has a great resource—their Water Filtration Guide—that helps you navigate your water filtration choices (www.ewg.org/tapwater/water-filter-guide.php).

No More Plastic Water Bottles

Plastic bottles are bad for you and for the environment, yet Americans drank 12.8 billion gallons of bottled water in 2016 according to a study by the Beverage Marketing Corporation, and only one-fifth of those bottles were recycled. The assumption is that the water is cleaner, yet an EWG study in 2008 showed that much of that water bore the same properties as tap water. And bottled water has fewer regulations for toxins and contaminates than tap water.

The most important thing I do and ask everyone I know to do is to *not buy* water in plastic bottles. Refusing to buy water in plastic bottles is the easiest way to start living with a green heart. It has health and environmental benefits by keeping the toxins found in plastic out of your body, our landfills, and our waterways. All plastic has some level of petroleum in it. Exposure to these petrochemicals have been linked to hormone and endocrine system disruption. While scientists and doctors don't know the extent of the effects these endocrine disrupters have on your body, over a prolonged period of time they have been known to increase your risks for cardiovascular disease, breast and prostate cancer, early puberty, obesity, diabetes, infertility, erectile dysfunction, and learning and attention-related disorders.

Not only is the water in plastic bottles not good for you, but transporting bottled water takes a lot of fuel. Additionally, the plastic bottle never completely breaks down. Decaying plastic slowly and eventually grinds down to small microscopic bits of plastic called microplastics, which have been found in every water supply in the world, from oceans to tap water. These microplastics wind up in fish and other marine life and eventually on your dinner table. For a deeper dive into the myth of bottled water, I suggest reading foremost expert, Peter Gleick's book: *The Story Behind Our Obsession With Bottled Water*.

Over the years, I have amassed a wide supply of reusable water bottles. My preference is a refillable glass water bottle. My second choice is a high-quality stainless steel bottle. Not all metal water bottles are created equal; make sure your bottle is 100 percent high-grade stainless steel and not aluminum; many aluminum bottles have liners made of bisphenol A (BPA), which can be harmful, especially in children. The same detective work goes for plastic reusable water bottles.

Most now claim they are BPA-free, but make sure they aren't using an alternative compound instead. Lids and bottle tops may also contain these toxins.

If you are "on-the-go," there are some new disposable drinking water options that are coming into the market, like Boxed Water and Just Water, which is also boxed and uses a plant-based biodegradable cap. The actor and singer Jaden Smith is one of my environmental heroes for coming up with this concept as a teenager and then making it happen.

Conserve Water

As a California resident who has been living through a drought since 2011, I am ever mindful of conserving water. We'll talk more about using gray water and tips on how to conserve water later in the book, but being mindful of simple things like turning off the faucet when

---

RefusePlastic

According to *The Guardian*, there are one million plastic water bottles purchased every minute, that's almost twenty thousand every second of the day. The most impactful thing you can do as an individual is to refuse to buy water in plastic bottles. Fewer plastic water bottles being used means less plastic in our water. This also means refusing other drinks in plastic containers. And please, please join Adrian Grenier in his "STOPSUCKING" campaign and refuse plastic straws. There are good paper alternatives now like Aardvark or the world's first edible, hypercompostable drinking straw, the LOLISTRAW.

Think Before You Flush

In 1999 and 2000, a US Geological Survey report found low levels of pharmaceuticals, including antibiotics, hormones, contraceptives, and steroids, in 80 percent of the rivers and streams it sampled. While much of that contamination comes from health institutions and pharmaceutical plants, people who do not properly dispose of unused medications also contribute to the problem. One of the recommendations in the guidelines for proper drug disposal from the US Food and Drug Administration (FDA) is to see if there is a community drug take-back program in your area.

---

brushing your teeth, making sure that your taps are not dripping, and checking that your toilets are not leaking has a great impact and is not to be underestimated. EWG also has a great section in their *Healthy Living: Home Guide* dedicated to water efficiency.

Our bodies are 60 percent water. The planet is 70 percent water. Of this water, only .007 percent is fresh and accessible to the human population. Water lubricates our joints, regulates our body temperature, and helps to flush out waste. Gandhi survived for three weeks without food, but without water we can survive only three to four days. You can find out how much water your household uses at the US Geological Survey's website, water.usgs.gov/edu/activity-percapita.php, if your water report does not have a usage chart attached..

Green Heart Actions

- Test your tap water.
- Get a water filter or purification systems for all water entry points of your home.

Eco-Hero: Robert F. Kennedy, Jr.

The Waterkeeper movement was started by Robert F. Kennedy, Jr., and a band of blue-collar fishermen on New York's Hudson River in 1966. Their tough, grassroots brand of environmental activism sparked the river's miraculous recovery and inspired others to launch local Waterkeeper groups around the world.

Today, Waterkeeper Alliance unites more than 300 Waterkeeper Organizations and Affiliates that are on the frontlines of the global water crisis, patrolling and protecting more than 2.5 million square miles of rivers, lakes, and coastal waterways on 6 continents.

Waterkeeper Organizations and Affiliates defend the fundamental human right to drinkable, fishable, and swimmable waters from the Great Lakes to the Himalayas, and combine firsthand knowledge of their waterways with an unwavering commitment to the rights of their communities.

- Conserve water.
- Don't buy water in plastic bottles.
- Join the Plastic Coalition (www.plasticpollutioncoalition.org).

EMFs

---

*I choose to be in a quiet and
creative state of mind every day.*

I met a woman who told me she slept with her cell phone under her pillow, and she was surprised when I told her that was probably the reason she wasn't sleeping very well. I explained to her that while technology is a great connector, allows us to stay close with others no matter where they are in the world, and keeps us from getting lost as long as there's a Wi-Fi connection for our GPS, it does have its drawbacks. What she hadn't thought about and most of us don't realize is that technology is also connecting us with increasingly high levels of man-made electromagnetic fields, commonly referred to as EMFs.

EMFs can occur naturally in the environment as a result of the buildup of electric charges that are present after a thunderstorm. We don't think about them because we can't see them with the human eye, but these invisible fields are what make a compass right itself. We've never had to worry much about the effect they might have on our health because until now the bulk of these EMFs were produced naturally and our exposure was minimal. Technology has changed all that. The introduction of the iPhone in 2007 and the subsequent increase in the use of mobile technology was just the beginning.

There are two types of man-made EMFs. ELFs are extremely low-frequency radiation, or alternating-current magnetic fields that are produced during electric power generation, transmission, and use. These fields decline pretty quickly the farther they get from their source, which is why close proximity to a power plant is more dangerous than proximity to the outlet you plug your lamp into.

The second type of EMF, and the one that is more concerning given our increased use of technology, is radio frequency (RF) fields. This form of radiation is produced from the use of mobile devices, including telephones, computers, televisions, radio, Wi-Fi, and Bluetooth. And because of increased use of wireless technology that is rarely turned off, these types of EMFs are more difficult to get away from than ever before.

Because this is a twenty-first century invention, we don't know everything about what the long-term effects of EMFs will be, but we do know there are real dangers to our health.

In 2011, the WHO's International Agency for Research on Cancer classified cell phone and wireless radiation as a "class 2B Possible Human Carcinogen" based on studies that showed long-term users of cell phones had higher rates of brain cancer on the side of the head where they usually hold their phone. Some studies have shown that cell phones damage sperm when the phone is carried in a pocket or attached to a belt and may cause cancer when tucked inside a bra. Other studies have shown that cell phone use alters brain activity and how the brain consumes glucose. And we know children are at increased risk. A study done by an oncologist, Dr. Lennart Hardell, in Sweden found that those who started using a cell phone as teenagers developed brain cancer four to eight times more often than those who did not. The Environmental Health Trust released a paper in the fall of 2018, further confirming the connection between cell phone use and cancer.

No matter what study you look at, there's no disputing that cell phone use alone, which the comScore reports to be 78.8 hours a month; a little under two hours and thirty minutes a day for adults, has contributed to an enormous increase in our exposure to EMFs. It is important to note that the weaker the signal indicated on the cell phone display, the stronger the signal the cell phone puts out. And the stronger the signal, the greater the amount of radiation that's being delivered to your body. Dr. Devra Davis says that—if possible—it's best to stick to a landline or to use the speakerphone function or use a headset when the signal is weak.

Scientists at EMFscientist.org, which include Martin Blank, Ph.D., Columbia, Magda Havas, Ph.D., Trent University, Henry Lai, Ph.D., University of Washington, Ronald Melnick, Ph.D., former senior scientist, NIEHS/National Toxicology Program, Joel Moskowitz, Ph.D., UC Berkeley, and Annie J. Sasco, MD, DRPH, University of Bordeaux, see enough evidence of increased cancer risks, cellular stress, genetic damages, changes in the reproductive system, learning and memory deficits, and neurological disorders that they have issued an appeal to the United Nations, the WHO, and the United Nations Environment Programme (UNEP) for greater health protection. They also see EMFs as harmful to plants and animals. Sensitivities can be unspecific, too, such as lack of sleep, poor concentration, and irritability or the person in general. We're long past the point where we can eliminate our use of technology. It's a part of how we live, work, and play, but there are things we can do to minimize our risks to the short- and long-term effects of EMFs by making health-conscious decisions. For more information, I highly recommend watching *Generation Zapped* directed by my friend, Sabine El Gemayel.

Start with Testing the Areas
Where You Spend a Lot of Time

Your first action is to test all your spaces for exposure, but start with where you lay your head at night. Your bedroom is probably the room in your house where you spend the most time, and it's while you sleep that the body heals and regenerates itself. You can hire an expert to come to the house or invest in a gauss meter, which costs about $150. A gauss meter will measure all the radiation levels in your home. A safe level should be in the 0.1–0.5 milligauss range.

Remediation

If your radiation levels are high, you can purchase an EMF Home Remediation Kit through EMF Solutions. If you can remodel, I recommend using Armored Cable or MX Cable between the frames and behind the drywall. In the past, Romex Cable was used, which did not have electric field shielding. It's interesting to note that it is now code to have shielding on the cables in commercial buildings, but not in residential buildings. Shielding material can also be applied behind drywall if Romex Cable was used.

Shielding

There are lots of shielding materials available today, such as window treatments, window film and wire meshes, roofing materials, and shielding paint. Shielding paint is particularly effective when used on the wall behind your bed to block out outside frequencies.

Source removal would be your next best action; however, most of us need a light next to our beds, but you can work with an electrician to have a "kill switch" installed to turn off the electricity in specific rooms such as all the bedrooms and the room where your wireless router is situated. I've done this in my home, and the only way I can describe what it feels like to sleep in a room when all the electricity is off, is that it's like being in a power failure, so peaceful you can hear yourself think.

Creating Confines

If opening walls and calling an electrician isn't in the cards, creating barriers between you and your sources is the next best option. Most of us—myself included—are usually searching for a Wi-Fi connection, but did you know that even when you're not using your Wi-Fi, it continues to draw power and emit EMFs? One easy and quick fix to minimize exposure is to turn off your Wi-Fi when it's not in use. Every computer and mobile device has a function to turn off the Wi-Fi.

You should also be cognizant of the EMF emissions from the routers themselves, which vary depending on the brand your provider uses. Keeping your body ideally at a distance of forty feet from the router, but at a minimum of ten feet will minimize your exposure and shouldn't impact your Wi-Fi connection. Putting your router on a timer is an even better idea, and there is actually new software available today that will allow it to turn off and on by itself. There are very few of us who can do this during the day, but try to do it at night as excess radiation can also disturb your sleep. I also recommend checking to see where your Wi-Fi router is and making sure it's not close to the bedroom, as walls will not block wireless radiation. A great solution would be to move your router to your garage, your attic, or as far away as you can put it. To further protect bedrooms, a shielding material like a high-frequency shielding paint is great when applied on the walls pointed in the direction of the router. This will stop any frequencies entering your bedroom from the direction of the router.

Keep your phone at least three feet away from your head, or you can do as Arianna Huffington suggests in her book *Sleep Revolution* create a charging station for your phones in another room. I know many people like to use their phone as an alarm clock, but consider investing in an old-fashioned battery-operated (or even wind-up) one.

Switching your phone to airplane mode will stop the microwave radiation emissions when it's not in use, but will not eliminate lower-frequency magnetic fields. You can also check with your Internet provider to learn how to manually control the signal strength coming

Practice Safe Cell Phone Use

- Live by the "golden arm rule" and keep all electronics at least three feet away from your head.
- Don't carry your phone close to your body—in your pocket or bra—where it's close to vital organs.
- Look for cell phone cases that lower radiation, like the Pong Case. You can also add a Cell Phone GemAlign energy balancer to the back of your case.
- Use the speaker function or airtube headsets.
- Turn the power off at night or use airplane mode. Your alarm will still work.
- Avoid using your phone in metal-contained spaces like moving vehicles and elevators where radiation exposure is higher and is transmitted to other people.
- Text instead of calling.
- Try not to download large files or images.
- Avoid using your cell phone when there are only a few bars.

into your home. Unplug small devices when they're not in use so they're not using standby energy, and don't leave chargers plugged into the wall when they're not plugged into your device as that increases your exposure.

Internet-ization Is Going to Make Things Worse

As more and more of our devices become connected, we will have more exposure to EMFs. Voice-activated assistants like Alexa or Google Home may be helpful, but they are using Wi-Fi, and when Wi-Fi is used, the amount of EMF radiation emitted increases. It's a wonderful convenience to be able to turn the air-conditioning in your home on before you've left the office, but keep in mind, when adding these gadgets to your life, you are enabling the Wi-Fi connections and exposing yourself to more radiation.

Make the Best Choices When It Comes to Utilities

Many people have a choice of utility providers, and within those utility providers a choice of renewable energies. If possible, try to add solar panels to your home. One of the biggest benefits of solar energy is that it results in very few air pollutants. An analysis by the National Renewable Energy Laboratory found that widespread adoption of solar energy would significantly reduce levels of nitrous oxides, sulfur dioxide, and particulate matter emissions, all of which can cause health problems. The laboratory found that, among other health benefits, solar power results in fewer cases of chronic bronchitis, respiratory and cardiovascular problems, and lost workdays related to health issues.

Although some utility companies are putting smart meters on homes to monitor the amount of electricity, that's not a good idea from an EMF point of view, as they often emit high levels of EMFs.

Walk Barefoot in the Grass

This is one of my favorite habits. While it does not stop EMFs from being transmitted, alternative medical practitioners recommend walking barefoot in nature. This practice allows you to ground into the earth and helps to absorb the free electrons. It also helps to naturally detoxify electromagnetic radiation. According to physicist Richard Feynman in his lectures on electromagnetism, when the body potential is the same as the Earth's electric potential (grounded), it becomes an extension of the Earth's gigantic electric system. The Earth's potential thus becomes the "working agent that cancels, reduces, or pushes away electric fields from the body". Plus, it feels good!

Green Heart Actions

- Test the radiation level in your home. .
- Use the golden arm rule to keep electronics away from your head.
- Keep your Wi-Fi router a minimum of ten feet, ideally forty feet, away from you and shut it down at night.
- Use headphones or the speaker function *always* when using your cell phones and use a landline for long conversations, if available.
- Unplug small countertop appliances and chargers when not in use and turn off power strips when not in use.
- Walk barefoot in the grass to detoxify the EMFs.
- Buy high-quality EMF-safe earbuds.

PERSONAL CARE

I choose to use healthy products
that respect my body.

M Y MOTHER WAS A SKIN DRILL SERGEANT. She was obsessed with the way that I took care of my skin, which was so annoying when I was a teenager. Nonetheless, I followed her lead. It wasn't until many years later, when I was regularly complimented on how healthy my skin looked, that I became grateful for her insistence. She taught me early on the importance of personal care and how the way we take care of ourselves and our bodies can determine the quality, and often the longevity, of our lives.

Good environmental hygiene is one of the best ways to care for our bodies. What I have learned is that it is not just the act of washing our hands or shampooing our hair on a regular basis that matters, the personal-care products we choose are also important. Unfortunately, if we are not paying attention, we may be doing more harm than good by choosing products that are loaded with chemicals and toxins and slowly poisoning ourselves and the planet in the process. We need to carefully read labels and not be fooled by words like *natural*, or which are often marketing attempts to "greenwash" a product that is not as healthy as it says it is. And we can't even really depend on ingredient labels. Although the Fair Packaging and Labeling Act requires cosmetics and personal-care products to have an "ingredient declaration" that lists the ingredients used in the product, the law cannot force a company to disclose "trade secrets" like fragrance and flavors. This loophole is where manufacturers can hide chemicals and other toxins that are not good for your health or that of the planet. Upwards of 3000 chemicals can be labeled "fragrance," hundreds of which are known toxicants, allergens and irritants, according to Heather Patisaul, Professor Biological Sciences Center for Human Health and the Environment, WM Keck Center for Behavioral Biology NC State University.

A study conducted by the EWG showed that the average adult uses nine personal-care products with a total of 126 unique chemical ingredients! (www.ewg.org/skindeep/2004/06/15/exposures-add-up-survey-results) More than a quarter of all women and one out of every one hundred men use at least fifteen products daily. That is a lot of chemicals potentially being absorbed through your skin and getting into your bloodstream. The next sections are intended to aid you in making better choices in personal-care products. Choosing better personal care products is one of the easiest ways to reduce your body's toxic load. You don't always have control over the chemicals that you are exposed to in your environment, but you have complete control over the products you buy and use on your body. You are likely not going to get cancer from using a bad moisturizer once, but a lifetime of exposures can have profound negatives effects.

The Truth About Toothpaste

Practicing good oral hygiene
gives me something to smile about.

My dad was an orthodontist. He taught me at a very young age that your teeth and gums are a window to your overall well-being. A good dentist can spot signs of disease. Inflamed gums can indicate higher levels of cortisol due to stress. Pale pink gums may be a sign of anemia. Frequent mouth infections at the root of the tooth can indicate diabetes. Sore red spots may be a sign of autoimmune diseases such as lupus or Crohn's disease. Chronic inflammation has been associated with heart problems. Antidepressants and antihistamines can cause dry mouth, reducing the amount of saliva, which is our body's natural protection for our teeth.

Regular trips to the dentist and good brushing are essential to good hygiene and personal health. Daily brushing and flossing can keep bacteria under control, but as is the case of most personal-care products, not just any toothpaste or mouthwash will do.

Use the Right Toothpaste

The first thing most of us do in the morning, aside from looking at our smartphones, is brush our teeth. What we should also be doing is reading the label on the toothpaste brand we've chosen. Many contain triclosan, an endocrine disruptor that has now been banned in hand soaps and body washes but is still in some toothpastes and some other personal-care products. Fluoride is added to strengthen teeth and control the acidity in your mouth; however, fluoride should never be swallowed. It is a chemical that can accumulate in your system over time and has been linked to neurological and endocrine dysfunctions. Be careful of propylene glycol, a mineral oil used in many personal-care products, that is sometimes added to toothpaste as a surfactant to make it easier to apply. This is the same type of mineral oil used in antifreeze and airplane deicers. You definitely do not want this in your mouth. Teeth whiteners may make for a prettier smile, but can often contain lead and other heavy metals. Sodium lauryl sulfate is a chemical added to toothpaste to create the foaming action that can cause canker sores, bad breath or bring out existing allergies. If you do insist on using a product with fluoride or other nonorganic ingredients, please rinse your mouth with water two or three times to get out as much of the leftover residue as possible.

A lot of personal-care products, including toothpaste, contain additives for texture and color, such as microbeads, most commonly listed as polyethylene on the label. These tiny plastic pellets often go unnoticed; however, they can get stuck in your gums, trapping bacteria with the potential to cause gingivitis. As we discussed in the section on water, these microplastics are not only highly destructive to you but to the environment, eventually making their way into our water supply, where they are mistaken as food by fish and act as a sponge for pesticides and heavy metals.

Organic toothpaste is best. Tom's of Maine and Dr. Brite tooth-pastes are available at health food stores and even some drugstores. Most recently, I have been using Davids. They use the highest quality ingredients, no fluoride or sulfates, and sustainable packaging.

Choose the Right Toothbrush

The type of toothbrush you use is another vital consideration. If you must use a toothbrush made of plastic, make sure both the handle and the bristles are free of BPA, polyvinyl chloride (PVC), and phthalates. My recommendation is to look for a toothbrush with natural bristles.

Bio-Toothbrush

Upward of two billion plastic toothbrushes end up in the oceans and the landfills every year. I recommend that you use a plant-based bamboo toothbrush. My favorite organic-certified, BPA-free, castor bean oil bristle, 100 percent bamboo brush is manufactured and distributed by Clean Planetware. It is a US Department of Agriculture (USDA)–certified biobased product, and the company is a Green America–certified business.

I do floss regularly and love Dr. Tung's Smart Floss. Instead of the petrochemical wax found on most floss, this brand uses a natural blend of vegetable wax and beeswax. The dispenser is also biodegradable.

Brush Your Tongue

I didn't know what brushing my tongue meant until the dentist pointed out how white my tongue was one day and said, "See that? That's bacteria. It will cause cavities." Please brush your tongue at the end of every brushing to keep it clean, too. A healthy tongue is a nice pink tongue.

Chose a Chemical-Free Mouthwash

Choose a chemical-free mouthwash made without alcohol. My favorite is Dental Herb Company's Tooth & Gums Tonic. It contains pure essential oils and has healthyl ingredients like extract of echinacea, gotu kola, cinnamon bark, eucalyptus, and lavender. It also contains no animal ingredients and has not been tested on animals.

If you are feeling even more adventurous, you might want to try "coconut oil pulling". Coconut oil pulls out bacteria and toxins from the mouth. Just swish around one or two tablespoons of high-quality organic coconut oil first thing in the morning. Keep the oil in your mouth for ten to twenty minutes and then spit the oil out into a trashcan. (You don't want to spit in the sink because when the coconut oil hardens it can clog the drain.) Then rinse your mouth with water and brush your teeth. Really, it could be called "oil swishing," as the word *pulling* can be confusing, but it refers to the idea that the oil is pulling bacteria and toxins out of the gums. *Streptococcus mutans* is one of the bacteria that are prominent in the mouth, and it has been studied for its role in tooth decay and gum disease. Oil pulling has been shown to reduce the level of *Streptococcus mutans* in the mouth, especially when done with coconut oil. Some benefits of oil pulling include reducing bad breath, healing gums, reducing inflammation, and preventing cavities. Some people believe it also boosts your immune system.

Find the Right Dentist

If your mouth is the window to your health, your dentist has the best view, so choose wisely. I gravitate toward doctors who take a holistic approach to medicine. The materials a dentist uses are as important as his or her skills. Traditional amalgam fillings can contain mercury, which is dangerous to your health. A good biological or holistic dentist will choose biocompatible materials that are better for the patient and the planet. My dentist, Dr. Chester Yokoyama, is SMART certified (in the Safe Mercury Amalgam Removal Technique) by the International Academy of Oral Medicine and Toxicology, which means that he follows the protocol for the safe removal of mercury amalgams. Dentists who take a green heart approach will also be conscious of having a sustainable practice. Every time I go into Dr. Yokoyama's office, he shows me his latest eco-friendly purchase; he even has a water-free vacuum system that he uses to suck away the water as you swish it out of your mouth. It can save up to 480 gallons of water a day. He is doing his part to help California to conserve water, and just think of how California's water supply could benefit if all dentists were to choose a water-free vacuum system!

Green Heart Actions

- Choose a biological/holistic dentist.
- Buy a toothpaste that has the USDA organic seal and doesn't contain triclosan, propylene glycol, or sodium lauryl sulfate.

- Always use organic dental floss and remember to brush your tongue.
- Choose a chemical-free mouthwash made without alcohol.

Deodorant

I am filled with gratitude
and love for my body.

Brushing my teeth is not my only morning ritual. I do a Shambhavi meditation , three sun salutations, and say my intentions before coffee. I also try to do one hundred sit-ups and fifty push-ups, go to a yoga class, take a jog in the flats, or hike in the mountains three to

---

Antibacterial Essential Oils That Smell Good

- Geranium
- Lavender
- Lemon
- Lemongrass
- Tea tree
- Thyme

---

four times a week to work up a good sweat. Sweating not only feels great, but is also good for you. When our body temperature rises, we automatically perspire, releasing salty sweat that allows us to naturally cool down. We are born with between two and four million sweat glands and a body naturally designed to sweat, yet drugstore shelves are loaded with antiperspirants to stop us from letting these glands function naturally.

Say No to Antiperspirants

The choice between a deodorant and an antiperspirant is not a choice. You never want to apply a product to your skin that inhibits your body from performing a natural function like sweating and naturally eliminating toxins. If that is not enough to convince you, listen to this: aluminum can be found in most antiperspirants. The concern here is that this is a metal that has been linked to "gene instability," in breast tissue, and has been found in brains of patients with Alzheimer's.

Use an Organic, Chemical-Free Deodorant

Many of the chemicals used in deodorants can make their way past your skin and into your bloodstream. Be especially careful to not apply chemical-containing products under your arms after shaving, when the skin may be broken; the likelihood the chemical will wind up in your bloodstream can increase. I would advise you to never apply anything under your arms within twenty-four hours of shaving.

The biggest chemical offenders in deodorant are parabens, triclosan, phthalates, and fragrance.

Parabens, as you will learn throughout this book, run rampant in personal-care products. Their purpose is to work as a preservative to extend shelf life, but they are also known endocrine disruptors that like to play games with your hormones. This is of special concern in the case of deodorant, which is being applied so close to breast tissue and your lymph glands, where it could help to grow cancer cells. According to professor of biological science, Heather Patisaul, parabens, which are notorious endocrine disruptors, have been found in breast cancer tumor samples removed from patients. Although "being at the scene of the crime" does not mean a compound or compound class is "guilty" of causing harm, more than 1000 studies in a variety of models have shown that parabens are likely enhancing the risk of breast cancer, sperm damage, and other adverse outcomes in reproductive tissues.

Phthalates, other chemicals commonly found in personal care, are added to make the deodorant stick. Unfortunately, what might also stick is their ability to disrupt your endocrine system.

Triclosan, the endocrine disruptor that was discussed in the previous chapter on toothpaste, while banned in antibacterial soaps, may still be showing up in your deodorant, so it's important to check those labels.

The last toxin-containing substance to be aware of in the case of deodorant, and the most commonly overlooked, is fragrance, which doesn't sound very toxic at all, but is the catchall where manufacturers can hide the chemicals they don't want you to know about.

DIY Deodorant

Combine 1/4 cup baking soda with 10–20 drops of the antibacterial essential oil of your choice and mix well in a small mason jar. Apply after showering, patting the deodorant under your arms instead of rubbing it in, until it is no longer visible.

Natural essential oils should be the only scent in your deodorant. I especially like products that use antibacterial essential oils, such as lemongrass and lavender. It's not your sweat that smells bad. It's the combination of your sweat with bacteria. Antibacterial oils kill the bacteria that cause the odor. My favorite deodorant brand is Freedom. My daughter Katie likes Schmidt's Charcoal + Magnesium, a mineral-enriched deodorant. Another favorite is the Primally Pure Charcoal Deodorant.

Green Heart Actions

- Say yes to sweat.
- Choose deodorants over antiperspirants.
- Choose organic deodorant brands that are free of parabens, aluminum, triclosan, phthalates, and synthetic fragrance.

Soap

I have a clean body and a healthy mind.

Our skin is the largest organ, spanning an area of approximately twenty square feet and weighing about eight pounds. It protects us from germs and from the elements. It allows the sensations of hot and cold and of touch. It helps to regulate our body temperature. What we put on it—including soaps, lotions, cosmetics, and

---

Organic Soap Brands

- Everyone Hand Soap
- Soap for Goodness Sake
- Makes 3 Organics
- Look for small-batch shops online at Etsy or at local farmers' markets

---

fragrance—is absorbed into our systems. That means that if what we're putting on our bodies contains harmful chemicals, those toxins are seeping under our skin and can become the source of health problems.

As with all personal-care products, always choose one that says "organic" in the labeling and is fragrance free or naturally scented. If you can't pronounce or don't know the first three words listed in the ingredients, you don't want to put it on your body.

Beware the Chemicals That May Be Hiding in Your Soap

Our obsession with cleanliness, fueled by advertising campaigns that stigmatize body odor and germs, has created a culture dependent on soap, overriding the fact that the soap we choose to use has as much an effect on our health as the microbes that we are trying to wash away. Most of us think of pesticides when it comes to spraying for bugs, but pesticides have been added to many soap products, in particular antibacterial soaps, which contain antimicrobial pesticides. Historically, these pesticides were used to inhibit the growth of or kill bacteria, fungi, or viruses that caused infectious diseases, most commonly in medical settings. However, today they may show up in the form of triclosan, a pesticide that disrupts thyroid function and reproductive hormones. In September 2016, the FDA put a ban on the use of triclosan in soap products; however, triclosan may still appear in other personal-care products, so take note and avoid it.

While this ban is a step in the right direction, it's important to know that it does not preclude the fact that many toxic substances are hidden in what is called the "the fragrance loophole," as previously mentioned. According to Heather Patisaul, professor of biological sciences at the W. M. Keck Center for Behavioral Biology, upward of three thousand chemicals can be labeled as "fragrance," hundreds of which are known toxicants, allergens, and irritants. The word *perfume* may sound innocent, but it is a place to hide many of these substances that give personal-care products texture, fragrance, and shelf life without identifying the chemical by name.

Stay Away from Antibacterial Soap

The notion that we should be bacteria free at all times is not good for our health. There are also good bacteria, and unfortunately, many of the antibacterial soap products on the market also kill the good stuff, affecting our immune systems and our ability to fight real infection. Studies show that children growing up in too sterile an environment have higher rates of allergies and asthma.

Choose Bar Soap over Liquid Soap

Living with a green heart is about choices that are healthy for us and for the planet, which is why I highly recommend forgoing liquid soaps. Liquid soap makes approximately a 25 percent larger carbon footprint than bar soap. Liquid soap production uses more energy in both production and packaging, which is generally in those plastic bottles that the Earth is incapable of digesting. A bar of soap completely disappears when it's finished. Plus, we use an average of seven times more liquid soap than bar soap every time we go to the sink. I have banned all liquid hand soaps and body washes in my house. My favorite gift to give or receive is a beautiful bar of handmade soap from the farmers' market or a cottage workshop.

Green Heart Actions

- Buy organic bar soap.
- Avoid buying hand soap in plastic bottles.
- Avoid buying any bar or liquid soap with a fragrance. A rule of thumb: if you can't pronounce an ingredient, don't put it on your body.
- When drying your hands (after washing), use a towel to avoid the waste of paper towels, or air dry.

Hair Care

My hair reflects my inner beauty.

While I can cut out sugar, conventional meat, processed foods, bottled water, soda, chewing gum, buttered popcorn at the movies, and almost everything else, I cannot forgo my eco–blow-dryer and the quarterly visits to Fabrice and David, to get a cut and some blond tint woven into my hair to complement the gray that is rapidly appearing. As I said at the beginning of this book, living with a green heart is a personal journey for which we all make individual choices, and none of us, including myself, will lead a perfectly eco-friendly life. However, beyond my hair-tint vice, there are other ways I choose to go greener when it comes to hair care.

Use Hair-Care Products Free of Chemicals

Shampoo, conditioners, hair-care products, and dyes fall under the FDA's definition of cosmetics, "articles intended to be rubbed,

poured, sprinkled, or sprayed on, introduced into, or otherwise applied to the human body for cleansing, beautifying, promoting
attractiveness, or altering appearances." And the cosmetics industry
is largely self-regulated in the United States. New products and ingredients, with the exception of color additives, do not need
approval before they show up on your drugstore shelf. The FDA issues guidelines and expects companies to check the safety of their
products before sale, but there is no direct oversight. European
countries are much stricter in their standards. The US Center for
Environmental Health reports that there are more than 1,300 chemicals banned from personal-care products in Europe, compared with
a mere eleven in the United States.

So, what should you look for when choosing hair products?
There are three main things to avoid: fragrances, certain preservatives, and sulfate surfactants. "Fragrance," as we've already
discussed, is where you may find chemicals that can be toxic, so try
to find shampoos and conditioners that are naturally scented.

Parabens and formaldehyde-releasing preservatives are added to
products to extend the amount of time the product can sit on the
shelf, and they can be harmful, linked to endocrine disruption and
reproductive and developmental toxicities. As we've already discussed, parabens are added to many personal-care products as a
preservative to improve shelf life. They may show up on a list of ingredients as methyl paraben, ethyl paraben, propyl paraben, butyl
paraben, isobutyl paraben, or E216. What all those forms have in
common is that they are known hormone disruptors and have been
linked to many cancers, including breast cancer. Shampoos, conditioners, hair sprays, styling products, dyes, and salon treatments like
popular hair straighteners are full of parabens.

Surfactants are in products to create suds. Sulfate surfactants are
added under many names, including sodium laurel sulfate (SLS) and
sodium laureth sulfate (SLES). Sulfates are what create the suds and

leave hair feeling clean and free of oils; however, there is some controversy surrounding their use. Most beauty magazines recommend avoiding sulfates because they can dry out your hair, and—if you have color-treated hair—they can cause the color to fade. But the green issue with sulfates is due to their origin. Sulfates are produced from petroleum or from a plant source such as palm and coconut oil. The production of petroleum products is associated with climate change, pollution, and greenhouse gases. Even those surfactants made with palm oil can be problematic due to the destruction caused by palm tree plantations.

Plus, all these chemicals get washed down the drain and are dumped into the streams and oceans in which your children swim and fish live.

The good news is that there is a wide selection of organic hair-care products that are made from plant extracts, including avocado and argan oils. Some brands to look for are Reverie, Rahua, John Masters Organics, and 100% Pure. And I am happy to say that as I write this I am consulting with some master hair experts to open a revolutionary new approach to hair care in Santa Monica. My new favorite product is BODE and was co-created by Paul Kephart and Brian Bode. I can't wait for it to be widely available. Using it makes my hair look great and I feel much better knowing I'm not hurting the fish.

Healthy Living App and the Skin Deep Database

One of my favorite resources in EWG's Healthy Living App, which is powered by their Skin Deep Database. This allows you to search a product by name or scan by barcode. It will give you a list of ingredients plus EWG's safety rating

Choose Your Hair Salon Carefully

Hair salons are hot spots for harmful chemicals. Hair dyes, particularly those that darken hair, contain phenylenediamine, a coal tar derivative and a known human carcinogen. Many hair straighteners don't contain formaldehyde but they do contain methylene glycol, which even at the low levels of 0.2 percent is not considered to be safe. Others include fragrances, methylisothiazolinone, iodopropynl butlcarbamate and SD alcohol 408. Not only are these ingredients bad for you, but when treated with a flat iron they can turn into a toxic gas which is then released into the atmosphere. These chemical straighteners have been banned in many countries, but to date they are still legal in the United States

In the interest of their customers' and their own health, many hair salon owners are now self-regulating and are choosing products from a growling list of organic brands. They are also looking for ways to green-up their methods of business by repurposing, recycling, and capturing the enormous amount of salon and spa waste. Green Circle Salons have created a movement with a goal to make all their certified salons 100 percent sustainable businesses by 2020.

Green Heart Actions

- Choose hair products or treatments based on what they don't have: harsh chemicals, sulfates, or parabens. EWG-verified is a great way to start.
- Choose a hairbrush with natural bristles.
- Look for certified Green Circle Salons.

Sun Protection

I allow the sun to nourish my body.

The sun debate is a hot one. Whether we're talking about indulging ourselves with a day at the beach, hiking in the desert, or just going about our everyday activities, we are in the path of the sun's rays. There is the camp that advocates staying out of the sun completely, while others believe that a controlled amount of direct exposure while suitably protected is the better option. I fall into the latter camp; however, I am vigilant about my sun exposure. I always apply sunscreen to my face in the morning as part of my skin-care routine. And as much as possible, I try to plan my outdoor activities either early in the morning or late in the afternoon; the sun is the strongest between 11:00 A.M. and 3:00 P.M., so I try not to spend a lot of time outside then. I do have a weakness for hats, possibly because my beloved grandfather always wore one, so you will never find me outside without a hat, especially when I am sitting outside for hours on end watching my daughter ride at a horse show. Even at the beach, you will find me wearing a loose long-sleeve cover-up and sitting under an umbrella. But there is more to know about sun protection than wearing long sleeves and sitting in the shade.

When I was growing up, sun lotions tended to focus on enhancing your tan with minimal protection. Today, sun protection is needed on a daily basis. The reason has everything to do with the breaking down of the ozone layer.

Ozone is a gas that exists in a layer in the upper atmosphere to protect the Earth from the harmful ultraviolet radiation of the sun, so we can receive the benefits of sunlight. Air pollution and the release of chlorine and bromine into the atmosphere from industrial production are breaking down the ozone layer. Not only is that harmful to humans, it also has its effect on the Earth and all its creatures. This extra ultraviolet B radiation inhibits the reproductive cycles of single-celled organisms like plankton and algae as well as those of young fish, shrimp, crab, frogs, and salamanders, and it disrupts the food chain.

Choose the Right Sunscreen

There is no question that you will need a higher level of protection for prolonged sun exposure, but don't assume that the higher the sun protection factor (SPF) number the better. According to the American Academy of Dermatology, once you get to SPF 50 the difference in protection is minimal. What is important is that you reapply the sunscreen every two hours.

You will want to look for a broad spectrum SPF product that includes both ultraviolet A (UVA) and ultraviolet B (UVB) protection. UVB rays are the ones that cause the superficial burning that we can see; UVA rays penetrate deeper, causing skin aging and DNA damage. Both are linked to skin cancer.

Here's what you need to watch out for: while you're protecting your skin, you could also be exposing it to other additives that can create new health hazards.

The FDA has not reviewed evidence of potential hazards of sunscreen filters; instead it grandfathered in ingredients used in the late 1970s, when it began to consider sunscreen safety. However, here's what we do know:

Arabenzone and oxybenzone are commonly found in sunscreens. Both have been found to be unstable and possibly have destructive molecules that can harm your cells and trigger early aging and cancer.

When I told you earlier that parabens were everywhere in personal-care products, I was not kidding. The more you are in the habit of reading labels, the more you will notice that these endocrine disruptors are loaded into many sunscreens, body and face creams, and lotions.

Para-aminobenzoic acid, commonly known as PABA, is an organic compound that blocks out harmful ultraviolet rays of the sun when added to sunscreen and topically applied; however, that benefit may be outweighed by the potential side effects. Clinical

---

Recommended Sunscreen Brands

- All Terrain
- Attitude
- Badger
- Bare Republic
- Goddess Garden

dermatologists say that prolonged use of PABA can cause skin abnormalities, including discoloration and cancer. PABA protects you from carcinoma, but not from melanoma.

Mineral oils, often labeled as petroleum, paraffin, and petrolatum, do more than make your skin feel softer. According to the EWG, petroleum-based ingredients readily penetrate the skin, and the *Journal of Women's Health* published a report in 2011 that stated, "There is strong evidence that mineral oil hydrocarbons are the greatest contaminant of the human body." (www.ewg.org/news/news-releases/2007/02/08/ewg-research-shows-22-percent-all-cosmetics-may-be-contaminated-cancer) Not only that, petroleum-based products also are classified as xenoestrogens—chemicals that imitate estrogen—and are linked to hormone imbalance. Further, they don't allow your skin to breathe. Applying mineral oil products is like wrapping yourself in plastic wrap, and that's just not healthy for your skin.

Once again, the good news is that the range of organic products made with natural ingredients continues to grow. Know what to look for and what to avoid, including synthetic fragrance and perfumes, which is where manufacturers often hide the stuff they don't want us to know about.

Zinc Oxide Is Your Best Protection from the Sun

Zinc oxide sits on your skin and serves as a physical block to the sun. It literally bounces the light back into the stratosphere. A thick layer of it on your nose may remind you of the lifeguard who sat outside in the sun all day, but you'll be happy to know that zinc oxide is an ingredient in many of the best and safest sunscreen products.

Don't Use a Spray Sunscreen

Spray aerosols have been popular in many personal-care and household products in the last fifty years. Chlorofluorocarbons (CFCs) are the chemicals commonly found in these sprays and are a chief reason why the ozone layer is breaking down. When CFCs reach the upper atmosphere and are exposed to UVA rays they break down to other substances. One of these substances is chlorine, which when it reacts with oxygen atoms in ozone tears apart the ozone molecules.

Sun Exposure in Moderation Is a Good Thing

One of the good things about sun exposure is that it allows us to naturally produce vitamin D, which is essential for the health of our immune, brain, and nervous systems. Vitamin D breaks down quickly, so we constantly need to replenish it.

There is a growing concern that the increased presence of SPFs in skin lotions and creams studies are contributing to vitamin D deficiencies. It's important to note that vitamin D levels are not always included in standard blood panel tests, so if you're interested in knowing whether or not you are deficient, you might need to request it the next time you get a blood test. There are two ways to address a Vitamin D deficiency: take supplements and allow yourself ten minutes a day, a few times a week, of unprotected time in the sun.

Green Heart Actions

- Avoid the sun from 11:00 a.m. to 3:00 p.m.
- Always wear a hat with a brim that covers your face.

- Wear a lightweight long-sleeve shirt and pants if all-day sun exposure is unavoidable.
- Check out EWG's Guide to Sunscreens for safety ratings. Avoid chemicals such as parabens, oxybenzone, and PABA. (www.ewg .org/sunscreen)
- Use a non-aerosol sunscreen.
- Thoroughly wash your face and body at the end of the day if you have been wearing sunscreen.

Makeup and Moisturizers

My face radiates happiness and love.

Our obsession with cosmetics to enhance our beauty dates back thousands of years to the ancient Egyptians, who used burnt matches to darken eyes, berries to stain lips, and copper and lead ore for color and definition. The Roman philosopher Plautus once said, "A woman without paint is like food without salt," a remark that sounds pretty sexist in today's world and was not how I was raised. The culture of the sixties favored a more natural look for women, as did the philosophy of Sweet Briar, the woman's college I attended. As a result, I am not very good at putting on makeup, and try to get by using as little as I can.

The beauty and personal-care industry is estimated at $78 billion in the United States alone, so it is in their best interests for them to get you to buy their products, but not necessarily yours. Whether you choose to wear a lot of makeup or the bare minimum, as I do, it is important to know what's in that makeup before your put it on your skin.

Choose Your Makeup Wisely

Although we think of cosmetics as topical applications, their ingredients don't just remain on the surface of the skin; they also are absorbed into our bloodstreams and eventually, when washed off, sent into our water waste streams. If our makeup contains dangerous chemicals, it is not good for our health or the health of marine life.

Lipsticks have been criticized for having lead in them. In 2007, the Campaign for Safe Cosmetics published a report on a study called "A Poisoned Kiss: The Problem of Lead in Lipstick," which called out lipstick manufacturers for the lead and other toxins found in commonly used lipsticks. In 2009, the FDA released a follow-up study that found lead in all the samples of lipstick tested, at levels ranging from 0.09 to 3.06 parts per million, which were even higher than those found by the Campaign for Safe Cosmetics. Many medical experts agree that any exposure to lead is unhealthy. Face makeup is full of the same synthetic mineral oils, phthalates, and parabens found in sunscreens, shampoos, and conditioners. Many also contain siloxanes, which are endocrine disruptors that can affect the reproductive system. One of the main ingredients in eye shadow is talc, a suspected carcinogenic linked to ovarian cancers. Eye shadow often also contains coal tar, a substance banned in the European Union but still in use in North America and linked to organ system toxicity and skin tumors. Petroleum distillates, produced side by side in oil refineries that produce automobile fuel and heating oil, are some of the ingredients commonly found in mascara, and we've already discussed the problems with petroleum. Butylated compounds known as BHT and BHA are endocrine disruptors and are often added as preservatives to eyeliners, eye shadows, lipsticks, lip glosses, blushes, and foundations. Their links to organ, developmental, and reproductive toxicity have caused the European

Makeup Brands to Look For

- Axiology
- Beauty Counter
- Juice Beauty
- lilah b.
- W3LL People

Union to also ban them from products. Unfortunately, they have not been banned in the United States.

Although I think a natural look is the most beautiful, if you do want to use cosmetics, there are some things to look for. While a USDA Certified Organic label is a plus, it's important to note that use of the word *organic* is not regulated by the FDA and the USDA when it comes to personal-care products, as it is in other industries. The same goes for words like *eco*, *natural*, and *nontoxic*. Manufacturers can use these words without proof. However, if a product does carry the USDA Certified Organic seal, it means the product ingredients were regulated. The key is to stay informed and always read labels.

Fortunately, there are some great resources to help you make the best, most informed cosmetic choices. Think Dirty is an app that lets you scan a product's barcode to get to information about the ingredients in the product. The EWG has the Skin Deep Database, which catalogs more than seventy thousand products. Skin Deep rates each product on a scale from 1 to 10, with 1 to 2 considered "low hazard." You can also check the Campaign for Safe Cosmetics' Red List (www.SafeCosmetics.org) and Made Safe's website (www.madesafe.org).

Healthy Moisturizing Brands

• Attitude
• Biossance (bonus—they have a plant-derived retinol alternative)
• Primally Pure
• True Botanicals
• Women's Heritage

Alternatives to Moisturizers

We all want our skin to stay moist and dewy looking, but we also want to be careful about what we use to keep it hydrated. In the case of moisturizers, in addition to the usual toxic suspects like fragrance and parabens, moisturizers generally contain mineral oils and/or paraffin. The problem with these ingredients is that they are not good for our health or our environment. And while they may feel nice on your skin, they can actually clog our pores, inhibiting our skin's ability to breathe.

Use the resources listed above to find the best skin-care options, or just go to your local supermarket or health food store and pick up some organic coconut oil or 100 percent almond oil. You can mois-

Moisturizing Tip

Try dry brushing your skin to slough off dead skin cells and then apply a thick layer of coconut oil before you jump in the shower. You'll be amazed how little moisturizer you need post rinse.

turize your skin safely and effectively for a fraction of the cost of high-end products. There are a lot of new CBD inspired products coming into the beauty marketplace which are probably worth checking out, if you are so inclined.

Be Careful with Antiaging Products, Skin Lighteners, and Acne Products

David Bowie once said, "Aging is an extraordinary process where you become the person you always should have been." Unfortunately, many of us don't want that aging to show up on our face. The result is a market flooded with skin-care products to help us not look our age, but in the process they can spur a host of diseases. Retinyl compounds may stop the appearance of a fine line or two, but will also speed the development of skin tumors and lesions on sun-exposed skin. A report in 2015 from the Breast Cancer Fund's Campaign for Safe Cosmetics discovered that a toxic contaminant, perfluorooctanoic acid (PFOA), which has been linked to cancer, was found in antiaging products. PFOA is a contaminant of polytetrafluoroethylene (PTFE), an ingredient that is used not only in personal-care products but also to create a smooth finish on cookware.

Once again, the rule of thumb is that if it is a synthetic material you cannot pronounce, you don't want it on your skin.

Skin lighteners are controversial, and I don't recommend them, but the ingredient to look out for in skin-lightening products is hydroquinone, a suspected carcinogen that is banned in Europe, Japan, and Australia. This ingredient has also been found to cause ochronosis (dark discoloration of skin and other tissue) and often disfiguring and irreversible disease where the skin can become tough. Many skin lighteners also contain mercury and steroids, and the longer they are left on the skin, the higher the level of toxicity.

The FDA has issued warnings about the dangers of topical acne products containing ingredients such as benzoyl peroxide or salicylic acid, yet these products are still on the market. These toxins can cause rare but serious and potentially life-threatening allergic reactions or severe irritations. Triclosan, which we already discussed in the chapter on toothpaste, may also still be found in acne products.

Bare Nails Are Best

The polish that paints your toes a pretty shade of red might also contain what is referred to as the toxic trio: toluene, dibutyl phthalate, and formaldehyde, the last of which is a known human carcinogen. Polishes also usually contain triphenyl phosphate (TPHP), a hormone disruptor that has been linked to early onset of puberty, neurodevelopmental problems and obesity. This is especially a problem for our teens and tweens who are the most vulnerable. The nail industry estimates that nine out of ten girls between the ages of twelve and fourteen, use nail products, sometimes daily. TPHP can be found in the blood as quickly as ten to fourteen hours after painting, according to a study conducted by EWG and Duke University (www.ewg.org/release/duke-ewg-study-finds-toxic-nail-polish-chemical-women-s-bodies). Your best choice is to skip polish like I do, but if you must paint those toes, choose an organic polish.

No Bunny Needs to Be Harmed to Test Efficacy

No matter what the product, along with the ingredients on the package, I always take into consideration how sustainably the business is run, like whether or not they're taking steps in production to minimize waste and greenhouse gas emissions and to conserve water. In the case of cosmetics, I also want to know that the product is not being tested on animals. Leaping Bunny and eight other animal protection groups joined forces to create an international standard and symbol to look for (a stylized leaping bunny logo). They've also designed a handy app that you can download and check on the go.

Green Heart Actions

- Remove from your makeup bag all products with toxic ingredients such as phthalates or any others you can't pronounce.
- Check EWG's Healthy Living App and the Safe Cosmetics or Made Safe websites for ratings and the latest in organic skin-care products.
- Try going without makeup once a week.

Intimate Care Products

I choose to care for my body,
my partner, and my planet.

The last thing that is likely to be on your mind when engaging in an intimate moment with your partner is the chemicals in the lubricant you may be using or the spermicide added to a condom; however, as in everything you put on or in your body—including sanitary products—there are safer green, healthier options.

Forgo Fancy Washes and Cleaners

Our culture has us obsessed with cleanliness and odor, especially when it comes to our private parts. Drugstore shelves are filled with feminine wipes, washes, and douches, all loaded with dyes, fragrance, and chemicals like butlyparaben and ethylparaben, which have been linked to cancer, infertility, neurological defects, and endocrine disruption.

What you may not know is that the vagina is naturally designed to be self-cleaning. Nothing more than a little water and an occasional mild natural soap are needed to maintain a healthy ecosystem there. A lot of vaginal infections are self-induced because of the use of the very same bath products, washes, and douches marketed to keep it clean and odor free.

Manage Menstruation the Green Way

The first disposable sanitary pads are said to be an invention of nurses on the battlefields of France. They made them out of wood pulp to stop the excessive bleeding of wounded soldiers during the late 1800s. Johnson & Johnson later created their version in 1896 and called it Lister's Towel: Sanitary Towels for Ladies. Today, the average woman throws away 250 to 300 pounds of tampons and sanitary pads in her lifetime. Close to twenty billion sanitary napkins, tampons, and applicators are dumped into North American landfills every year. When wrapped in plastic bags, feminine hygiene waste can take centuries to biodegrade. However, this colossal waste burden isn't the only ecological impact of disposable feminine hygiene products. A life-cycle assessment of tampons conducted by the Royal Institute of Technology in Stockholm found that one of the largest impacts on global warming was caused by the processing of LDPE (low-density polyethylene, a thermoplastic made from the monomer ethylene) used in tampon applicators as well as in the plastic backstrip of a sanitary napkin, which requires high amounts of fossil fuel–generated energy.

Further, the majority of the products made today include dioxins and furans from the chemical bleaching process, both of which are known human carcinogens. Many products also contain bleach, pesticide residues, and chemical fragrances. There is nothing very green when a toxic product is first inserted into a woman's vagina and then later winds up in a landfill, contaminating soil.

We can't stop the natural flow of a woman's cycle, but we can do something about the products we use to manage it. You might be growing weary of hearing me say this, but choosing organic is the green heart approach. Fortunately, as more people wake up to the toxins being used in our manufacturing processes and the consequences they have on the environment, more products are coming to market that are organic and free of harmful chemical additives—and in the case of tampons, do not include plastic applicators. There are lot of organic tampons and sanitary napkin brands to choose from, so find one that fits your budget. But do make sure that they are free of dioxins, furans, and chemical chlorine bleaches.

For the adventurous woman, one great green option for menstruation is a menstrual cup that does not contain latex, plastic, PVC acrylic, BPA, phthalates, polyethylene, color, or dyes and is eco-friendly. Brands to look for are the Diva Cup, Lunette and Intimina Lily Cup. There are also organic period-proof undies like Thinx.

Be as Choosy About Your Condom and Lubricant as You Are About Your Partner

Condoms are a good thing. When used properly they can be effective in preventing sexually transmitted diseases and pregnancy. Lubricants can enhance sexual pleasure, but if you don't know what you're buying you may be harming your health in the process.

Intimate Care Brands to Check Out

- Brandless
- Cora
- Lola
- Natracare
- Sliquid Organics
- Sustain Natural
- This is L. Inc.

The majority of condoms are made with nitrosamine, a known carcinogen. Many condoms add in fragrance and flavors that are not friendly to either partner when absorbed by the skin. Another common additive is spermicide made with nonoxynol-9, a detergent that disrupts layers of the cell membranes.

Most lubricants are made with petroleum, propylene glycol, polyethylene glycol, glycerin fragrance, and parabens—all toxins we've discussed before that damage cell tissue, have been linked to endocrine disruption and cancer, and have no place being anywhere near your vagina.

Like finding a good partner, you may have to look a little harder for the condom and lubricant brands that are organic, natural, and produced without harmful chemicals, but they do exist. I highly recommend the brand Sustain Natural Condoms. A friend and an eco-giant, Jeffrey Hollender (founder of Seventh Generation) started the company with his daughter, Meika to be a "net positive business that plays a 'regenerative' role, both socially and environmentally, rather than just being 'less bad.'" Their brand, Sustain Natural, also offers organic sanitary products free of harmful chemicals, dyes, fragrances, and synthetics.

Green Heart Actions

- Choose an organic sanitary product with no bleach or opt to use a menstrual cup or Thinx.
- Choose an organic lubricant and condom free of fragrance.

FOOD AND BEVERAGES

I am one with all that I put in my body.

M ANY OF MY LESSONS LEARNED from living with a green heart have been learned the hard way. Such is the case with food. After having an eating disorder as a teenager, I had to learn how to eat again after college. When your mind has learned to override your body's hunger signals, it's very hard to get back in touch with how it feels to be hungry and what foods are good for you. Once my doctor explained to me that eating is fuel for the body, I dove into researching what nutrition was derived from different foods. After I started learning how different foods fed my body, l began to understand how vital is the link between how food is grown and how it affects my health and that of the planet.

Today, I look at my food choices by prioritizing what my body needs and then work backward. Dr. Phil Goglia, the nutritionist whom I discovered while I was pregnant with my daughter, creates an individualized food plan based on your budget, your lifestyle, and a blood sample taken from a fingertip prick to determine your body type. A typical diet is composed of proteins, fats, grains, vegetables, fruits, and other foods. A plan for how to balance those elements can be tailored to your body type to achieve your personal best state of well-being. Allergies and other medical conditions such as diabetes are also taken into consideration, as well as cultural or ethical beliefs. As I've stated before in this book, I do not believe in a one-size-fits-all approach to living life with a green heart, and that is certainly true when it comes to diets and nutritionists. There are many great doctors and nutritionists who I admire like Dr. Mark Hyman and Dr. Steven Gundry, who have written multiple books on health and nutrition. My diet borrows from them and others, always shifting a bit based on how I feel on a certain day or what is going on in my life at the time,or where I am. What is most important when it comes to food choice is for you to get to know your body so you can craft a diet that is right for you.

As we get into the next chapters, the one thing you will hear repeatedly is that it is not just what you eat that matters but also how that food is produced. Satish Kumar, in his book *Soil, Soul, Society: A New Trinity for Our Time*, talks about the necessity of healthy soil and how soil can help heal our planet. Soil is at the center of our universe, and the way in which food is grown is at the core of a healthy individual and a healthy society. However, many of the farming methods being used today are creating degenerate environments that are destroying that soil. It's something that has been going on for generations but has now been exacerbated due to some corporate farming practices and the wider use of chemicals in modern farming.

As our relationship to the farmers who produce our food grows more distant, it's important to understand why we must support those growers who have committed to producing food in a manner that regenerates the Earth. The Carbon Underground and Regenerative Agriculture Initiative at California State University, Chico, defines regenerative agriculture as "farming and grazing practices that, among other benefits, reverse climate change by rebuilding soil organic matter and restoring degraded soil biodiversity—resulting in both carbon drawdown and improving the water cycle." In his book, *Project Drawdown*, Paul Hawken promotes farming practices that draw carbon down into the soil one of his one hundred solutions to reduce climate change. Regenerative agriculture treats the land more holistically. Instead of focusing solely on crop yields, it takes an integrated approach to farming by nurturing the soil's natural tendencies rather than depleting them. Instead of pesticides, chemical fertilizers, fumigants, and genetically modified organisms (GMOs), regenerative agriculture uses a set of farming principles based on working with nature, rather than trying to control it.

Biodynamic farming is also gaining in popularity. By definition it is a holistic, ecological, and ethical approach to farming, gardening, food, and nutrition based on the spiritual insights and practical suggestions of the noted philosopher Rudolf Steiner. We'll talk more about biodynamic farming when we talk about wine, an area that is leading the way in this type of farming and is producing a superior product as a result.

While biodynamic and regenerative practices can go a long way in reversing the damage of over farming and can improve soil conditions, the biggest challenge to the planet posed by mass food production is water usage. It is estimated that agriculture accounts for more than 30 percent of our total water usage. Water maintains all living things, yet it is a rapidly dwindling resource. Supporting farms that are committed to regenerative and/or biodynamic farm-

Eco-Heroes: Ryland Engelhart and Finian Makepeace

Kiss the Ground's mission is to inspire global regeneration, starting with soil. In the spring of 2013, Ryland Engelhart, co-owner of Cafe Gratitude, heard about soil as a solution to climate change from Graeme Sait, a New Zealand farming educator.

Ryland learned that building healthy soil has the miraculous ability to sequester carbon from the atmosphere, and knew in his heart it was a story that had to be shared with the world. And it's not just carbon storage; the ways that soil stands to positively impact lives of billions worldwide are tangible and immediate: replenished water cycles, restored fertility, regenerated ecosystems. Ryland told Finian Makepeace, a childhood friend and professional musician, and together they began telling others about the power of Today, they are an NGO that has had over 50 million unique impressions with "Regenerative" content. They have influenced global thought leaders, major food brands and educational institutions. Their four programs include: Media, Farmer Scholarships, Education Curriculum and Advocacy. They have co-produced a feature length documentary film called Kiss The Ground, due out in 2019. knowledge of their waterways with an unwavering commitment to the rights of their communities.

ing practices in combination with good water and wastewater hygiene is truly an act of living with a green heart. Remember, vote with your dollar – shift market change towards responsible farming. The benefits will be felt by all, including animals.

Dairy

I choose to drink milk that is healthy for me.

I learned that not all dairy is equal through my love of cheese. Having been raised on grilled cheese sandwiches made with bright yellow cheese slices individually wrapped in plastic, the first time I ever tasted real Brie and Camembert I was flabbergasted that cheese could be so delicious. I was in Paris in 1983 during a gap year following college and I had hardly any money, so eating bread, cheese and chocolate became a staple of my diet (until I gained fifteen pounds and couldn't fit into any of my clothes). Most surprising to me was that despite the fact that I, like more than 50 percent of the population, am lactose intolerant, I could eat cheese in France without any side effects. To this day, I have given up eating cheese everywhere, except in Europe.

Nearly everyone I know who has spent time in Europe has noticed the difference in their dairy products, and I have heard a few theories as to why that may be. First, in many cases, cows in Europe are grass fed, which many believe has superior nutritional properties and produces a better tasting milk from grain-fed cows. Some believe the difference is due to the absence of recombinant bovine somatotropin (rBST)—a hormone given to cows, in part, to increase milk production, which is still widely used in the United States but has been banned in most European countries. Although there are different schools of thought on whether the use of rBST poses a health risk to humans, Europeans often cite that the hormone can cause unnecessary pain and discomfort to cows as a humane reason for not allowing its use. Finally, some attribute the unique taste to the use of a process known as ultrahigh temperature (UHT), which is an alternative to pasteurizing, which is the norm in the United States. An environmental benefit of UHT milk is that it has a much longer shelf life than pasteurized milk, since it is heated to 275 degrees Fahrenheit (versus 160 degrees Fahrenheit in pasteurization], so it doesn't require refrigeration until it is opened.

Whether or not dairy products in Europe truly do taste better, there is no doubt that there are benefits to their dairy practices for the well-being of the cows themselves. Like humans, cows produce milk after they have given birth. In Europe and other select countries (including some dairies in the United States), cows are allowed to get pregnant and lactate on a natural cycle, which means that those cows can only be milked for five or six months a year. Most dairy cows in the United States are artificially inseminated shortly after their first birthdays, lactate for ten months, then are artificially inseminated again so they can produce more milk.

Having had three children myself, the concept of being indefinitely pregnant is beyond incomprehensible to me, much less being so at the discretion of someone else for their financial benefit. So, it is totally understandable to me that a cow might feel continuously stressed out being pregnant all the time, which might affect the quality of her milk. This prolonged lactation period also affects the lifespan of a cow.

Always Choose Hormone-Free Organic Milk

In order to keep the cows pregnant and lactating, many dairy farms inject them full of hormones. Beyond the pain and anguish that cows treated with artificial hormones can suffer, there is also a concern about the negative impact these sex hormones might have on us. A study by Ganmaa Davaasambuu, a Harvard University researcher and an expert on milk-related illnesses, makes a correlation between use of sex hormones in milk and the increase of breast, ovarian, and testicular cancer in humans. I strongly encourage you not to buy milk unless it says "Hormone Free" on the label. Your life may depend upon it.

The best option we have in the United States is USDA-certified hormone-free organic milk. When dairy products bear that certified label, it means that no growth hormones or antibiotics have been given to the cow to increase milk production and that the cow has been fed only 100 percent organic food, has been pasture raised, and was not fed grain or grain byproducts. Unfortunately, this label doesn't mean cows weren't exposed to any other hormones; the law does not require farmers to record other drugs administered to cattle. Pesticides, polychlorinated biphenyls (PCBs), and dioxins are other examples of contaminants found in milk. These toxins do not readily leave the body and can eventually build to harmful levels that may

---

No Dairy Is 100 Percent Hormone Free

All animal-based milk, whether it comes from a cow, sheep, or goat, contains small levels of natural hormones, including estrogen and progesterone. Look for dairy products that are free of artificial hormones and non-dairy alternatives that are free of GMOs.

affect the immune, reproductive, and central nervous systems. PCBs and dioxins have also been linked to cancer.

Choose the Right Yogurt

Since yogurt is made from milk, it's important to look for a yogurt made with hormone-free milk. I consume a lot of yogurt because it's an easy healthy food to eat on the run, which as a working mom is most of my life. I appreciate fast, easy and healthy, and these days I'm eating sheep or goat yogurt. Traditionally, yogurt is made when milk is fermented with the bacteria *Lactobacillus bulgaricus* and *Streptococcus thermophilus*. These beneficial bacteria, also known as probiotics, help preserve yogurt and improve its taste. Probiotics help us to digest the milk sugar lactose, making yogurt often tolerable by those who can't eat other dairy foods. In addition to supporting digestion, research suggests that probiotics in yogurt may boost the functioning of the immune system.

Yogurt is also a great vegetarian source of protein, and Greek-style yogurt packs about double the protein of regular yogurt, thanks to its straining process, which removes the liquid whey along with some sugars. A 6-ounce cup of nonfat plain Stonyfield yogurt has 8 grams of protein and 12 grams of sugar. But a slightly smaller size (5.3 ounces) container of nonfat plain Greek yogurt has 15 grams of protein and 6 grams of sugar and about half the sodium (60 milligrams vs. 115 milligrams).

The second most important ingredient to look out for when choosing a yogurt is sugar. Yogurt isn't healthy if it's loaded with sugar. The average American's intake of added sugar has increased from 20 lbs (9 kg) of sugar per year in 1850 to more than 160 lbs (73 kg) per year by the early 2000s. Choose a yogurt that has no more than 15–25 grams of sugar; anything over that means sugar has been added.

Choose the Right Butter, Too

Butter is made from the solid components of milk that comes from cows, sheep, goats, buffalos, and other mammals. Therefore, the same hormone-free rule as with milk applies to all the butter you buy.

Butter is about 80 percent fat, 15 percent water, and 5 percent protein. There are several types of butter available on the market. The most commonly sold butter is sweet cream butter, which has a lighter and fresher taste and is made from pasteurized milk. Raw butter comes from unpasteurized milk and has a shorter shelf life (ten days). Cultured butter has a tangier taste and is made by allowing bacteria to ferment the sugars in the cream before churning it. Ghee, a staple of Ayurvedic cooking, is clarified butter and is made by heating up butter until the water evaporates off and the protein separates from the fat. Spreadable butters have oil added to them to make them easier to spread. Whipped butter is made by adding water into butter to make it more spreadable, without the added oil.

Nut butters and fruit butters have become more popular in recent years (I eat a nut butter almost every day) and are great alternatives to regular butter since they contain more protein, are tasty, and are easier to spread—or eat out of the jar with a spoon, as I have been known to do.

Should You Give Up Dairy?

There are those who believe a dairy-free diet is your healthiest option. In the United States alone there are fifty million people who are intolerant to lactose, and the sugar found in milk and milk products can also make them more difficult foods to digest. And there is evidence that supports the idea that the health benefits of milk are far fewer than the American Dairy Association has promoted over the last seventy years. Dr. Sidney Baker, a pediatrician and the author of *Detoxification and Healing*, is one of many doctors who say that humans have evolved beyond a need to consume animal milk. We are the only species that drinks milk after we are weaned, and there are much better ways to prevent osteoporosis, such as eating dark-green leafy vegetables and engaging in regular moderate-impact exercise.

Do your own research when it comes to dairy. Whether you drink it or not is your choice. However, keep in mind that when it comes to dairy, it's not necessarily the milk but rather how it was produced. You might also want to consider that some researchers are finding an increased link between cancer and casein, a protein found in milk.

Is Almond Milk the Answer?

In July 2018, *PBS News Hour* reported that "the FDA has plans to enforce a federal standard that defines 'milk' as coming from the milking of one or more healthy cows." Although this sounds like dairy lobbyists at work, I don't think it will affect those of us who prefer, by choice or otherwise, "milk alternatives." Almond milk is a healthy nondairy choice that has become so popular, it leads all of the nondairy options in terms of sales. It tastes great, and its creamy texture makes it an ideal alternative to cow's milk. Unfortunately, almond production is a water-intensive process: it requires 1.1 gallons of water to produce a single almond!

When you consider that California, a state that continues to suffer from the longest drought in history, is one of the biggest producers of almonds, you'll be happy to know that almond milk is not your only nondairy choice. Other milk alternatives to try include coconut, cashew, walnut, hazelnut, pea, soy, rice, and even hemp milk. Once again, I caution you that this is a personal choice, and you may need to try a few of these before you find the one that's right for you.

Do cows have a secret life?

One of my all-time favorite books is *The Secret Life of Cows*. In it the author and farmer Rosamund Young gives the reader a glimpse into how cows posses many of the same habits and tendencies we have as humans. "Cows can love, play games, bond and form strong lifelong friendships. They can sulk, hold grudges, have preferences and be vain." This she learned while looking after the family farm's herd on Kite's Nest Farm in Worcestershire, England.

Choose Sustainability

Living with a green heart is not just about making healthful choices for ourselves, it's also about making decisions that are good for the planet. Take water usage: it takes thirty gallons of water to make one glass of dairy milk, twenty-three gallons to make one glass of almond milk, and nine gallons to make one glass of soy milk. Also, be mindful of the greenhouse gas emissions—including methane—connected to the production of animal-based dairy. Coconut milk has the smallest carbon footprint, followed by soy and almond milk.

Green Heart Actions

- Choose "Certified Organic" milk and cheeses produced without additives such as antibiotics or artificial hormones like rBST.
- Consider alternatives to cow's milk such as sheep's and goat's milk, or milk made from nondiary sources like nuts, coconut, or soy.
- If you shop at a farmers' market, look for cheese and butter made by a local farmer that is organic. Locally grown and bought is a double hitter!

Red Meat

I honor the life of cows.

When I was growing up in Kentucky, red meat was a staple on our dinner table, but then I had a brush with ovarian cancer and learned that estrogen can feed cancer cells and that eliminating estrogen-based proteins like red meat from my diet was something to consider. Since then, I made the switch to a plant-based diet with little to no dairy and a piece of sustainable fish every now and then to alleviate boredom.

Eating a plant-based diet has worked for me for the past five years; however, eliminating red meat from one's diet is not the answer for everyone. Vegetarians and vegans will advocate eliminating red meat completely; others will state that it is the quantity and the kind of beef consumed that is the issue. Eating meat is a personal choice, but what kind of meat is an environmental and health choice, for both you and the planet.

The WHO has stated that high levels of consumption of red meat, especially processed meat, may increase the risks of stroke and cancers and, in one report, identified bacon and sausage as carcinogens. Studies have found that people who ate the most red meat were 20 percent more likely to die of cancer and 27 percent more likely to die of heart disease. For women, the rate of cardiovascular-related death was 50 percent higher.

Beyond the health risks, the bigger-picture problem is the carbon footprint of beef production. Western countries, in general, consume more red meat than the rest of the world, with the United States leading the pack. Americans consume 60 percent more red meat than Europeans, and production is expected to double by 2050 to approximately 1.2 trillion pounds of meat a year! Raising cattle is another water-intensive industry. According to *Foodtank News*, the total amount of water needed to produce one pound of beef is 1,799 gallons. As a comparison, one pound of pork takes 576 gallons of water. The water footprint of soybeans is 216 gallons per pound, and for corn it's 108 gallons per pound.

The environmental impact of the meat industry goes beyond the strain on our water resources. According to the EWG's Meat Eater's Guide, growing livestock in the United States requires 149 million acres of land, 167 million pounds of pesticides, and 17 billion pounds of nitrogen fertilizer every year just to grow the grains to feed the animals (www.ewg.org/meateatersguide). The fertilizer applied to the soil emits nitrous oxide, a greenhouse gas that contributes three hundred times more harmful effects than CO_2 to the warming of the planet.

The pesticides and fertilizers used in raising cattle, including toxins such as nitrogen, phosphorus, and ammonia, run off into our groundwater, ending up in rivers, streams, and eventually the ocean.

Waste management also poses a risk to resources, including our water and air. While manure can be a helpful nutrient for plants, it can also leach pollutants into the groundwater, including any antibiotics the cattle may have been fed. Dust, smog, odors, and toxic gases, including ammonia and hydrogen sulfide, are released into the air

> ## The Less Red Meat You Eat, the Lower Your Carbon Footprint
>
> Going meatless for just one day for a family of four is equivalent to taking your car off the road for nearly three months.

when cattle waste decomposes. It's estimated that the production of cattle emits 20 percent of all the United States' emissions of methane, a greenhouse gas twenty-five times more toxic that CO_2. Beef and lamb production are the biggest culprits.

The electricity used to run the slaughterhouses is another source of greenhouse gases. The resulting poor air quality affects workers and those living close by. This does not even take into consideration the often inhumane aspects of mass slaughtering.

Something you might not have thought of when cutting into a juicy steak is that four-fifths of the deforestation in the Amazon rainforest is a result of cattle ranching. Livestock production uses 70 percent of the agricultural land in the United States and 30 percent of the land surface of the planet, according to the Food and Agricultural Organization of the United Nations. Trees get in the way of cattle grazing.

The health and environmental issues associated with eating red meat are complex. As I've said, eating meat is a personal choice. If you do opt to eat it, here are some guidelines to follow:

Choose Grass-Fed, Pasture-Raised Organic Meats.

Yes, this quality of meat is more expensive, but this is your health we're talking about. If that's hard to find, check your farmer's market or try eatwild.com to find a local pasture-raised ranch near you. You can also purchase meat with buyranchdirect.com if you can't find anything local. Plus, if you do decide to eat meat, ideally you should eat less of it. Think of meat as a condiment, not a main dish; 50 to 75 percent of your plate should be vegetables! And it's best to have meat no more than one or two times a week, which I realize may be difficult for my ketogenic and paleo friends, but there are other fats out there besides animal fat.

On the positive side, organic, pasture-raised, and 100 percent grass-fed red meat is an excellent source of protein, vitamins, and nutrients, including iron, zinc, vitamins B_{12} and B6, and niacin. And it contributes a much smaller carbon footprint. Grass-fed operations that are well managed are better for the environment and more humane. Moving the animals on a regular basis spreads manure more evenly and helps to conserve soil and reduce erosion and water pollution. Free-range and pasture-raised cattle farmed without antibiotics reduce the risks of bacterial contamination and exposure to toxins from pesticides.

Avoid All Processed Meats

Stay away from processed meats. The International Agency for Research on Cancer (IARC) , the WHO's cancer agency, has identified processed meats as a probable carcinogen.

Prepare Your Meat the Right Way

The way we prepare meats is the key. High-temperature cooking like grilling, frying, smoking, or charring causes toxic byproducts. All of this leads to the production of compounds called polycyclic aromatic hydrocarbons (PAHs) and heterocyclic amines (HCAs), which

---

Meatless Mondays

The Meatless Monday movement was founded in 2003 by Sid Lerner and others at the Johns Hopkins Bloomberg School of Public Health. Today, it is active in forty-four countries and growing. According to Earthday.org, if all Americans ate no meat or cheese for just one day a week, it would be the equivalent of taking your car off the road for nearly three months.

---

studies have shown cause cancer in animals. Change your cooking methods to reduce your exposure of these toxic compounds. The same rule applies to poultry, fish, grains, and veggies. Cooking these foods at too-high a temperature can cause the same problems. Focus on lower-temperature, slow-cooking methods, such as baking, roasting, poaching, and stewing.

You Can Have Your Meat and Not Be a Carnivore

Plant-based meat options now exist. One of my favorites is the Impossible Burger, the brainchild of Pat Brown, a Stanford University professor and CEO of Impossible Foods. A collaborative team of scientists, engineers, chefs, and farmers has created a burger that tastes like meat but is made from plants. They were so intent on getting this right they even isolated heme, an iron-containing molecule that is the secret sauce to make this plant-based option smell, sizzle, bleed, and taste like red meat. Giving up a good, juicy, home-cooked hamburger was one of the hardest things I had to do, so I love the Impossible Burger. Thank you Fedele Bauccio for introducing me to this delicious alternative!

Green Heart Actions

- If you eat red meat, eat organic, farm-raised, grass-fed meat, in moderation.
- If you are feeling adventurous, try the Impossible Burger.
- Become a flexitarian—someone who eats a mostly plant-based diet, but sometimes eats meats, poultry, and fish .
- Avoid deli and processed meat.

Poultry

---

*I choose to consume healthy
food from happy animals.*

Modern farming practices have a major impact on the quality of the food we ingest and the health of the planet. Factory and industrialized farms raise large numbers of livestock, often under crowded and inhumane conditions. Their goal is to maximize production at minimal cost, with little to no concern for the welfare of the animals.

Patrick Holden, who founded the Sustainable Food Trust in 2011, is working hard to combat this. His belief is that our worsening human and environmental crises stem from the majority of today's farming methods, and his organization aims to influence policymakers to make changes globally. Without clear policies for sustainable food production and farming methods, environmentalists face a strong headwind to make an appreciable difference. Agriculture, like many other industries that are subject to regulation, is represented by lobbyists and industry organizations that can be self-serving. The Sustainable Food Trust believes that "policymakers will be empowered to act when there is sufficient pressure from informed public opinion." It's time to make our opinions heard. Thank you Patrick, Adele, and friends at The Sustainable Food Trust.

Poultry farming isn't much different from cattle farming. Chicken production *is* responsible for emitting smaller amounts of greenhouse gases than beef and dairy farming because it requires far less feed and chickens don't generate methane gases. And while chickens emit slightly smaller amounts of other gases than turkeys do, they use more energy and water than most other meat processing.

I first became aware of the environmental hazards of chicken farming after I got involved with Waterkeeper Alliance. In partnership with the EWG, they mapped out the locations of more than 6,500 concentrated animal-feeding operations in North Carolina, showing how the enormous waste was contaminating the air and water of rural residents (www.ewg.org/research/exposing-fields-filth).

The news about chicken on the personal health front isn't much better. Injecting animals with antibiotics to enhance their appeal to consumers is at the crux of what makes them unhealthy to eat. In 2017, when I watched the documentary *What the Health*, I learned that farmers were injecting chickens with antibiotics that would plump their breasts to the point where the chickens were unable to walk because their breasts had grown heavier than their legs could carry. The visual of those poor chickens still sickens me.

Chickenless Wednesday?

According to the Environmental Defense Fund, "If every American skipped one meal of chicken per week and substituted vegetables and grains, the carbon dioxide savings would be the same as taking more than half a million cars off of U.S. roads."

Consuming chicken can also make you sick. The high dosage of antibiotics that they are fed to make them grow faster, coupled with their crowded living conditions, leads to an increased risk of antibiotic-resistant bacteria.

The same could be said for eating turkey. The turkeys we eat today are not of the same variety as they were fifty years ago. Most are factory farmed in overcrowded conditions and are fed grain and supplements—including antibiotics—instead of being allowed to forage for bugs and grass the way nature intended. This is done to produce what is called the "broad-breasted white" variety. Like chickens, they are raised this way to produce breasts that are so enlarged the birds can no longer reproduce without artificial insemination.

Duck may be a more sustainable poultry option, mainly because the demand for duck meat is lower than for other poultry, so they are rarely raised on factory farms. And because ducks are foragers, they live off pests like bugs or snails instead of feed, so duck farms use fewer resources than chicken and turkey farms.

Only Eat Poultry That Is Certified Humane and Has a USDA Certified Organic Seal

A small step that each of us can take is to only purchase poultry that is raised humanely, responsibly, and sustainably, to create demand around those standards. The USDA Certified Organic seal is always your best bet. It's the only assurance that what you're eating was raised in healthy, low-stress conditions with freedom for the livestock to move and exercise and that they are fed 100 percent organic feed, with no additives or antibiotics.

Free range is an option, but that only means that the birds were allowed to roam free for a period of time. It does not necessarily mean they were never caged. Pasture-raised and grass-fed also sound great,

Pasture-Raised Is Healthier

According to the Rodale Institute, pasture-raised birds eat grasses and legumes that contain vitamin A and omega-3 fatty acids, nutrients that are known to reduce cholesterol. Pastured birds also have more access to adequate space, fresh air, sunshine, and exercise, and thus maintain better physical health than confined birds. (Pastured birds require no hormones or antibiotics unless faced with acute illness.) With more exercise, birds maintain a lower fat content, which is healthier for the bird and the consumer.

Join the Heritage Turkey Movement

Heritage Turkeys are raised outdoors without confinement and allowed to eat according to nature, not industry. Look for Beltsville Small White, Jersey Buff, Narragansett Standard Bronze, and White Holland varieties in the United States. They cost more, but heritage turkeys taste better, and the farming practices support genetically diverse turkeys and help the species to survive.

but unless there is a certification or you know the local farmer, that does not mean that the birds were not fed any supplements.

Green Heart Actions

- Choose poultry that is certified USDA organic, pasture raised, and antibiotic free.
- Look for chicken that is certified humanely raised and handled.

Eggs

I choose to see each day as a new beginning.

My son Alex, and his girlfriend Soraya, raise chickens in their backyard. I've learned from them that, depending on the breed of the hen, the color of a farm-fresh egg can naturally be white, brown, blue, or even green. So the color of the egg does not affect the nutritional value. The freshest and most nutritious eggs will have bright orange and plump yolks with perfectly clear whites, while those that are not will have pale yellow yolks with dull, speckled whites.

While eggs hatched locally by chickens raised in humane conditions and fed organically are the best to buy, unfortunately, most of us are not lucky enough to be living close to a local farm and find ourselves standing in the supermarket trying to make sense of the multitude of labels.

Buy Eggs from Organic
Pasture-Raised Chickens

An estimated 95 percent of all eggs in the United States are produced in conventional or battery-cage systems. These wire cages may hold six to ten laying hens and usually have automated feeding, watering, and egg-collecting systems. According to the United Egg Producers, conventional cage systems typically provide each laying hen an average of sixty-seven square inches of floor space. In some egg operations, hens have even less space.

Cage-Free and Free-Range
Sound Better Than They Are

The other 5 percent of eggs are produced in either cage-free or free-range systems. There are two principal types of cage-free systems: floor and aviary. In both of these models, laying hens have access to the barn or housing floor, and they are provided with nesting boxes for egg laying. Instead of cages, many are kept in multilevel aviaries that might allow them to spread their wings, but certainly not to roam free. Beak cutting is permitted with cage-free systems to reduce pecking injuries. The European Union has some regulations that cover cage-free eggs, but this is not so outside of the union.

Guidelines for "free-range chickens" varies from country to country. According to the USDA, free-range or free-roaming producers "must demonstrate to the Agency that the poultry has been allowed access to the outside." Little information is provided about living conditions, stocking density, and standard industry practices, which keeps the consumer and chickens literally in the dark. So, while cage-free and free-range might sound like the hens are free to roam, that is not necessarily so. These labels also do not preclude the use of antibiotics in feeding.

Even eggs marked as organic don't hold any guarantees. To meet the USDA organic certification, eggs must come "from uncaged hens, free to roam in their houses and have access to the outdoors." They should also be "fed an organic diet of feed produced without conventional pesticides or fertilizers." The tricky part here is how that "access to the outdoors" is interpreted.

So, what kind of eggs should you buy? The freshest, healthiest eggs come from hens raised under the most humane conditions, such as in the backyard of my son Alex and at local small farms. But when those are not an option, reach for pasture-raised eggs. Organic , pasture-raised eggs are the only truly free-range ones available. And according to a study by *Mother Earth News*, they are also the most healthful, with one-third less cholesterol, one-quarter less saturated fat, two-thirds more vitamin A, twice as many omega-3 fatty acids, three times as much Vitamin E, and seven times as much beta-carotene as conventionally raised eggs.

Green Heart Actions

- Support local farmers and choose organic, pasture-raised eggs.
- Look for the USDA Certified Organic seal.

Something Fishy About Fish

I protect our oceans, our rivers, and our fish.

When it comes to food, we tend to think of fish as one of our healthier choices. The American Heart Association suggests that we eat fish at least twice a week, as it is a high source of protein, low in saturated fats, and rich in omega-3 fatty acids. However, fish brings with it unique considerations, as I discovered when a blood panel test for heavy metals showed that I had too much mercury in my system and that an excess of tuna and swordfish in our diets was the culprit.

Robert F. Kennedy Jr. and his team of more than two hundred worldwide Waterkeepers, who work tirelessly to keep our waterways swimmable, drinkable, and fishable, have campaigned and written extensively over the past twenty years about the effects that polluted water have on our personal and collective environmental health. In Kennedy's movie *The Last Mountain*, he specifically explores the consequences of mining and burning coal and exposes the effects of coal industrial practices. One major problem is that coal-fired electricity

---

Fish with the Highest Levels of Mercury

- Ahi tuna
- Bigeye tuna
- Bluefish
- King mackerel
- Marlin
- Orange roughy
- Shark
- Swordfish

---

and waste incineration increase the amount of airborne mercury. That mercury eventually finds its way into rivers, lakes, and oceans, where it is ingested by fish and other aquatic life. Once it makes its way into the marine food chain, a process called bioaccumulation occurs, which basically means that the mercury that the fish ate multiplies. That's not good for the fish nor is it good for those of us who eat the fish.

Too much mercury can be toxic to our nervous, digestive, and immune systems, as well as our lungs, kidneys, skin, and eyes. It's particularly dangerous in the development of young children and in utero, which is why pregnant women are advised to avoid exposure to mercury, which will bioaccumulate in your body over time.

In addition to the mercury in our seafood, we also have to worry about the plastic. I talked before about the plastic waste that winds up in the ocean, where it's broken down into tiny microplastics and consumed by fish. Did you know that by 2050 the oceans will contain more plastic than fish? According to the Plastic Pollution Coalition, even the tiniest ocean creatures are eating toxic microplastics, which ultimately throws off the entire aquatic food chain. And this in turn is leading to a decreased fish population, which is certainly not helped by overfishing. About 150 million metric tons (or 330 billion pounds) of seafood were consumed in 2016. The health and wellness movement has caused an increased demand for healthier protein, which has resulted in waters being overfished to biologically unsustainable levels. Pollution plus overfishing equals a crisis.

Farm-Bred Fish May Offer a Solution

Aquaculture is a method of farming fish and other seafood. Fish farming is not a new practice, and you may have heard warnings about farm-raised fish, but it's the method in which fish are farmed that makes the difference. There are several organizations that have created standards for responsible and sustainable aquaculture. Best Aquatic Practices (BAP) certification is given through the Global Aquaculture Alliance, a nonprofit that advocates, educates, and provides leadership in responsible aquaculture. Friend of the Sea is a nongovernmental organization (NGO) founded by Dr. Paolo Bray with a mission to conserve marine habitats, and the organization now offers a certification for sustainable fisheries and aquaculture. The Marine Stewardship Council is an international nonprofit whose certification and eco-labeling program also work to promote sustainable fishing and save our oceans.

Best Fish Choices According to the Environmental Working Group

These options are high in omega-3 fatty acids, low in mercury, and sustainable:

- Atlantic mackerel
- Wild salmon
- Sardines
- Mussels
- Rainbow trout

To see where these fish are coming from, check (www.ewg.org/research/ewgs-good-seafood-guide/executive-summary).

So, should you buy wild-caught or farm-raised fish? I wish there was an easy answer. There are a lot of factors to consider, including what kind of fish you're buying and where it comes from.

Use the Seafood Watch App

I know this can sound overwhelming, so when it comes to seafood choices, I recommend that you download the Monterey Bay Aquarium Seafood Watch App. I have found it to be the best resource in providing the most up-to-date information on sustainable seafood. You can search by seafood type and geography to see what restaurants and businesses are partners in Seafood Watch. Because it is an app, it is with you wherever you go, so you can make sustainable choices at the grocery store and in restaurants. If wild seafood is hard to find in your area, try ordering from online options like Vital Choice (www.vitalchoice.com).

Green Heart Actions

- Choose to eat fish in moderation.
- Download the Monterey Bay Aquarium Seafood Watch App and the EWG Seafood Calculator (www.ewg.org/research/ewg-s-consumer-guide-seafood/seafood-calculator).
- Check out the EWG's Safe Fish Guide.
- Choose fish with a Best Aquatic Practices, Marine Stewardship Council, or Friend of the Sea certification.

Fruits and Vegetables

I choose to eat a plant-based diet.

I have been eating a plant-based diet for many years. A spectrum of colorful fruits and vegetables on my plate is what has worked best for my personal health and the health of my family. I am happy knowing that eating this way not only reduces my risks of heart disease and stroke and lowers my blood pressure but also fuels my body with phytochemicals that work as antioxidants, phytoestrogens, and anti-inflammatory agents to help prevent cancers and keep my blood sugar in check. It's also better for the planet and its creatures. Growing fruits and vegetables consumes far fewer resources and less energy than producing meat and dairy products.

Living in California makes this easier, as fresh fruit and vegetables seem to always be available in abundance, but that doesn't mean that all fruits and vegetables are equally green. How they are grown, the quality of the soil that they were grown in, the amount of pesticides and radiation they have been exposed to, and how far they have had to travel to get to your plate are all criteria for determining their relative nutritional and environmental value.

Recently, evidence of radiation has been found in vegetables along the Pacific Coast as a result of the Fukushima nuclear accident in Japan in 2011. It is a controversial subject, with some saying that the radiation levels are too low to cause harm, while others are convinced that the levels are sufficient to pose a health threat. As in many of these environmental health issues, the best choice for the planet and ourselves may not be the most obvious one. If you ask Murray, my homeopath, how to avoid radiation in vegetables, he might encourage you to consider buying veggies from South America, yet doing so would result in a much larger carbon footprint due to the shipping distance. It is a climate change conundrum but worth wrestling with to come up with your individual decision.

Read Labels Carefully

Being an informed consumer is the only way to make the best green heart choices. You need to read labels carefully and understand exactly what they mean.

Don't confuse the word *fresh* with *organic*. The FDA regulation for the use of the word *fresh*, is complex and does not mean that the food is preservative free. The term *fresh* just means that the food was in its raw state. The grower could have used approved pesticides or a mild chlorine or acid wash post-harvest.

You should also be careful when it comes to the use of the word *local*. The 2008 Farm Act reads that any food with a "local" label must be transported less than four hundred miles from where the product was produced. That means that the "local corn" in a grocery store in Richmond, Virginia, could have been grown in New Jersey.

Organic Agriculture Limits the Effects of Climate Change

Organic farmers are extremely dedicated to the excellent quality of their soil. Research from CCOF (a nonprofit organization that advances organic agriculture and the Rodale Institute, demonstrates that soil under organic production can remove about seven thousand pounds of CO_2 from the air each year through sequestration. Imagine the impact that more acres of organic production could have on the health of the planet if consumers demanded more organic foods.

Steer Clear of Pesticides and GMOs

Synthetic pesticides are toxic. They are harmful to farmworkers and their children. Heavy exposure has been linked to ADHD and lower IQs in children and to cancerous tumor development in adults. They also hurt the environment by contaminating the soil and disrupting the natural cycles of wildlife, including bees, which are essential to our food chain and are now in threat of extinction. (Louie Schwartzberg produced a great movie called *The Hidden Beauty of Pollination*. It has the most unbelievable footage of pollinators and will make you never want to swat at a bee again.)

GMOs are genetically modified organisms. Originally created to improve nutritional value and to make crops more durable and less susceptible to drought, GMOs are very controversial and have been linked to health issues, including allergies and organ toxicity. Sixty-four countries globally (including all of the European Union) require producers to label the use of GMOs in their products, but there are no equivalent USDA regulations. There is, however, the Non-GMO Project, a nonprofit organization created to educate consumers and verify that brands meet their non-GMO certification standards. Vendana Shiva is an organic seed advocate who has devoted her life to setting up native seed banks to preserve our world's food supply and rescue seeds from disappearance. My friends, award-winning documentary film makers Laurie and Bill Benenson introduced me to her in their movie, *Dirt! The Movie*. This is another environmental film not to miss.

Go Organic or Go Home

Reaching for the percent USDA Certified Organic seal once again is the best way to ensure that you're eating fruits and vegetables free of pesticides, chemical additives, and GMOs, as the organic regulations are more thoroughly vetted than the rules for most of the US food system. Dr. Phil Landrigan, American epidemiologist and pediatrician, believes that "Eating organic can reduce the amount of pesticides we ingest by 70 to 90 percent." The extra cost may seem off-putting, but it's the best long-term investment you can make for your health and the health of the planet.

The 2018 Dirty Dozen According to the Environmental Working Group's *Shopper's Guide to Pesticides in Produce*

1. Strawberries
2. Spinach
3. Nectarines
4. Apples
5. Grapes
6. Peaches
7. Cherries
8. Pears
9. Tomatoes
10. Celery
11. Potatoes
12. Sweet Bell Peppers & Hot Peppers

The Numbers on the Stickers on Your Vegetables and Fruits Mean Something

Those little stickers on your produce are called PLUs, which is short for "price look up," and they provide more information than what you're going to be charged. A five-digit number that starts with a 9 means the product is organic, four digits beginning with a 3 or a 4 means it's probably conventionally grown, and a five-digit code starting with an 8 means it's been genetically modified.

Sometimes Frozen May Be Your Best Option

It seems logical that fresh vegetables or fruits would be a healthier choice, but it turns out frozen ones can be just as healthy or even healthier and better for the environment. Produce that is frozen right at its peak could offer more nutrients than fresh produce that has sat on a truck and traveled hundreds of miles.

What's important to look for when choosing frozen produce is when and how it has been frozen. According to FDA guidelines, a label that says "fresh" implies there was no processing, and "fresh frozen" or "frozen fresh" means the produce was frozen after it was recently harvested. However, "frozen fresh" may also mean that the produce has been blanched before packaging—a process that strips away some of the nutrients. It's important to note also that none of these terms means that no pesticides were used in the growing process.

Canned vegetables and fruits generally use salt, sugar, and other chemicals in the canning process to preserve the produce. The cans often contain BPA liners, which can leach into the food and are best avoided. Use canned produce only as a last resort and look for BPA-

---

Eco-Hero: Driscoll's

BerryMex, one of Driscoll's strongest partners, began growing berries in the San Quintín Valley of Baja California in 2000. Although the Valley is known as one of the most important agricultural regions in Mexico, it is an arid, dry zone with little precipitation. Farmers rely solely on groundwater aquifers, which have suffered from salt water intrusion from prolonged drought. Recognizing the region's limitations and to reduce their reliance on groundwater aquifers, BerryMex constructed an ocean desalination plant. The project underwent extensive environmental and research studies wherein they discovered that the volcanic soil indigenous to the region, allowed for a unique intake of ocean water from the shoreline and an innovative approach to processing the brine water through injection wells that filter naturally by dispersing below the aquifer and blending into the current aquifer levels. BerryMex is now able to farm in a more sustainable and environmentally responsible manner while also safeguarding the regions natural groundwater resources.

---

free cans, which are becoming more common. I have canned foods only in my earthquake and emergency supplies.

Green Heart Actions

- A plant-based diet is the healthiest diet for you and the planet.
- Look for organic produce whenever possible.
- Go to the farmers' market, farms or farm carts as often as you can.
- Try starting a garden box to raise a few of your own vegetables.

Grains, Flours, and Pasta

Each bite I take is a kernel of wisdom.

Grains, particularly whole grains, are a great source of dietary fiber. Grains are used to make breads, pasta, cereals, and crackers, and they are a staple in many diets. The type of grain we eat and how that grain is processed has a bearing on our health and the environment. Sadly, 95 percent of the grains we consume are refined. Refined grains are stripped of their bran and germ and generally have less fiber and lower levels of the nutrients folate, riboflavin, and vitamins B_1, B_3, and B_5. The most heavily refined and processed wheat grains are what make up white flour. That does not mean that whole grains are not refined at all. A "whole grain" label means that at least 51 percent of the product was made with whole grains.

Skip the GMOs

GMOs also play a role when it comes to grains. As we already discussed, GMOs started out with good intentions—extending the shelf life of food. The first GMO food product approved by the FDA was the Flavr Savr tomato in 1992, which increased the firmness of the tomato and extended the shelf life by inhibiting the growth of a natural tomato protein. However, when the genes of food plants are scientifically altered, so is the food chain. Many GMO crops are resistant to herbicides, which can force farmers to spray large quantities of controversial chemicals like glyphosate to combat the resistance. Some medical studies have shown a link between gluten-related disorders and autism, Parkinson's disease, Alzheimer's disease, endocrine disruption, and birth defects, all related to the overuse of glyphosate on GMO crops.

In a green heart approach to living, I advocate choosing the purest, least processed, and most nutrient-dense options. That excludes food made with GMOs. Its better for the soil too.

Choosing Gluten-Free Will Not Improve the Environment

My grandmother used to bake homemade cinnamon rolls and bread. Whenever we visited her, the smells from her baking would waft down the hallway to our bedroom, waking us up each morning. To this day, a warm slice of freshly baked bread is hard for me to turn down. However, many of us do, and our reasons go beyond the caloric intake. More and more people are choosing to eliminate gluten from their diets. While I do not suffer from celiac disease, gluten makes me feel sleepy, so I avoid it unless napping is on my schedule.

Gluten-Free Substitutes For White and Wheat Flour*

- Almond flour
- Buckwheat flour
- Cauliflower flour
- Chickpea flour
- Coconut flour
- Oat flour
- Quinoa flour
- Rice flour
- Sprouted corn flour

*Make sure all flours are certified gluten free

We hear a lot about gluten-free options when it comes to breads and pasta. This has come about from a heightened awareness around celiac disease, an autoimmune disorder that attacks the small intestine when a sufferer eats gluten. For others, like myself, who are gluten sensitive, gluten just doesn't make us feel good; we feel full, bloated, tired, and even foggy-brained.

Gluten is the protein composite found in many grains. It provides structure for the flour, pasta, or bread that is made from a particular grain, essentially acting as the glue to hold the food together. Gluten can be found in wheat, barley, rye, oats, semolina, spelt, farina, faro, malt, and brewer's yeast—even in grains that are grown organically.

As popular as gluten-free products are at the moment, there is controversy over eliminating gluten from your diet completely if you are not gluten intolerant. Many gluten-free products replace gluten with sugar and are highly caloric, so read labels and make your choices based on what is best for your body to function at optimal health.

An Ancient Wheat

Eikorn is the oldest known wheat and has never been hybridized. It has a high content of protein, phosphorous, vitamin B_6, and potassium when compared with modern forms of wheat. It also has plenty of carotenoids—the natural red, yellow, or orange pigments that are found in many vegetables and fruits and in a few grains. Carotenoids contain medicinal properties that help in preventing serious diseases such as cancer. Because eikorn has never been hybridized, people who are gluten sensitive or gluten intolerant are often able to consume it. This does not mean that people with celiac disease are able to consume it.

If you do choose to forgo or avoid gluten, you may want to consider some gluten-free products made from hemp, almond, or chickpea flours. Ancient grains like quinoa or amaranth are healthy and taste great!

Green Heart Actions

- Choose to eat simple whole grains.
- Choose breads and pastas made with organic, Non-GMO Project-verified, sprouted or whole-grain flour without additives, preservers, or improvers. Or better yet, try baking a loaf on your own.
- To help your digestion and gut health, get tested to see if you have a gluten intolerance or sensitivity.

Plant-Based Proteins

I welcome the nourishment of plants.

Our bodies need protein. Protein builds and repairs tissues and produces enzymes, hormones, skin, bones, muscles, and cartilage. However, when most of us think of protein sources we think red meat, chicken, and fish, which, as we've already discussed, require an enormous amount of the Earth's resources to produce. When I changed to a plant-based diet, I was pleasantly surprised to find that there are plenty of foods that do not come from animals that I could eat as a protein source.

As Americans, we sometimes believe that more of a good thing is even better. We associate protein with energy and toned bodies, so we overindulge. The National Institutes of Health's recommended Dietary Reference Intake of protein is 0.8 grams per kilogram of body weight, which translates into 56 grams per day for the average sedentary man and 46 grams per day for a woman, and it is recommended that protein intake is spread out across all meals. However, the amount of protein intake needed to maintain your health will vary depending on your age, gender, weight, and activity levels. The USDA Food and Nutrition Information Center has an interactive calculator that will help you determine your own personal needs.

Whatever your needs, keep in mind that there are seven grams of protein in one ounce of meat. This means that an average woman or man only need to eat seven to eight ounces of protein a day. For reference, four ounces of meat is roughly the size of the palm of your hand. I suspect most of us can eat much more than that in one sitting.

We would need even less meat if we used plant-based foods as the source of our protein requirement. Lentils have almost eight grams of protein for a half cup, tofu has ten grams per half cup, and there are a whopping eighteen grams in a half cup of peanuts. As we've discussed, eating more plants keeps us healthy while reducing our carbon footprint—saving water and minimizing greenhouse emissions.

Eat a Variety of Plant Proteins

Some people claim that animal proteins are better than plant proteins or that you can't get "complete" proteins from plants. Here are the facts: Proteins are made up of amino acids. There are about twenty amino acids, and nine of them are "essential," meaning they can't be made by our body, we have to eat them. Proteins that contain all of these essential amino acids are considered complete proteins. Some believe that only animal proteins are complete and that plant proteins are incomplete unless you combine them a certain way. Others say you just need to eat a variety of plants, including fruits, vegetables, legumes, nuts, seeds, and soy foods. However, there are plant-based foods that are complete proteins; these include amaranth, buckwheat, hempseed, quinoa (my personal favorite), seaweed, and spirulina.

The Skinny on Soy

Soy protein is made from ground soybeans that have been de-hulled and defatted. It is considered a complete protein, containing all of the essential amino acids. However, soy does contain one of the highest concentrations of isoflavones, plant chemicals that bind to estrogen receptors, so if you have a history of estrogen-related health issues, you may want to stay away from it. You also may want to be wary of processed soy such as the type that can show up in a soy protein bar or soy burger.

Choose Your Plant-Based Protein Powder Carefully

A scoop of protein powder is a great addition to my morning smoothie, but I am careful about what kind of protein powder I choose. Once again, it's important to read labels. Many commercial plant-based protein powders are loaded with sugar, artificial sweeteners and colors, and nonorganic ingredients, which defeats the whole purpose of choosing a plant option. The other consideration is what your body can tolerate. For example, a plant-based protein powder that contains dandelion powder is not going to work for

Smooth Sources of Protein

Using a plant-based protein source in a smoothie is a good way to get a hit of energy and fulfill some of your protein needs, but it shouldn't be the only source of protein in your diet.

someone with allergies to ragweed. As I discussed at the beginning of this book, living with a green heart starts with knowing your body and your specific health needs and always reading labels.

Make Your Choice Organic and Responsibly Produced

With so many brands including plant-based proteins in their products, you want to look for those that are certified organic, non-GMO, and ethically and responsibly produced. Nutiva is a company I like that meets the certification for a California Green Business and operates zero-waste facilities powered by 100 percent renewable energies.

Katie's Recipe for a High-Protein Green Smoothie

My daughter Katie is the healthiest chef I know, and makes the best protein shakes. She combines the most unlikely ingredients and winds up with the most delicious smoothies. Here's one of my favorites:

1 large frozen banana
2 handfuls spinach
1½ cups almond milk
1 cup steamed, then frozen cauliflower
1 serving protein powder
1 teaspoon finely ground flax seeds
1 teaspoon chia seeds
1 tablespoon almond butter

Blend all ingredients on high-speed in a blender and enjoy!

Green Heart Actions

- Choose USDA-certified organic vegetables to amp up your protein intake.
- Use organic, minimally processed plant-based protein powders such as hemp and pea.
- Try an Impossible Burger or Beyond Meat for a plant-based burger.

Nuts and Seeds

---

*I make nuts and seeds a
part of my healthy diet.*

I was probably a squirrel in a past life. You will never ever, ever find me without a bag of nuts in my bag. Snacking, especially on the run, can be a challenge when you take the green heart approach to living, but nuts and seeds are a great option. A handful of nuts and seeds contains vitamins, minerals, proteins, and fiber and can quiet the hunger while decreasing inflammation and reducing cholesterol levels. A study conducted at Harvard University found that those who ate an ounce of nuts five or more times per week had a 14 percent lower risk of cardiovascular disease (defined as a heart attack or stroke, or death from cardiovascular disease) and a 20 percent lower risk of coronary heart disease (defined as a fatal or nonfatal heart attack or stroke) during the study period than those who never or almost never ate nuts. Although I prefer roasted nuts, which can sometimes take out some of the nutritional value, raw nuts, without salt or any additives, are better for you. Even better are sprouted nuts (made by soaking raw nuts in water overnight). On average, one ounce of nuts contains six grams of healthy protein.

Choosing the Nut That's Right for You

As with most food, this starts with taste. Each variety of nut has their own flavor and health benefit.

No matter which nuts you prefer, as with all food choices, you want to choose those that are grown organically and that are GMO free.

When you consider the green heart factor, know that some nuts make less of an environmental impact in harvesting then others. On average, four ounces of nuts are equal to the carbon emissions of driving a car one-half of a mile. Brazil nuts must be grown in rainforests and require the assistance of certain insects to pollinate. These insects are only present if the trees are growing wild. In this way, harvesting Brazil nuts helps to protect the rainforest. Hazelnuts require very little water to grow and are drought resistant. Their root system even helps to remove carbon from the atmosphere. Pecans, walnuts, and pistachios need the least amount of water to grow. Almonds are extremely water intensive, requiring 1.1 gallons of water

---

Weeding Out the Bad Seeds

Nuts and seeds are always best when chosen in their raw or sprouted state without any added salts or oils. However, when you're not sure about your prepackaged choice, go to the EWG website (www.ewg.org/foodscores), where they score food based on nutrition, ingredients, and processing methods, with 1 being the best and 10 the worst.

to produce a single almond. With 80 percent of the world's almonds coming from California, almonds have become quite controversial in light of the state's recent drought issue. However, when used as a protein source and compared with the 106 gallons of water used to produce one ounce of beef, the 23 gallons used to produce one ounce of almonds, takes on a new perspective.

Seeds for More Than Snacking

Like nuts, raw seeds grown organically are great sources of protein, minerals, zinc, fiber, Vitamin E, and monounsaturated fats. Pumpkin seeds are high in omega-3 fatty acids and zinc, phytosterols that help stabilize cholesterol levels, and carotenoids that increase immune activity and fight disease. Also, among my favorites are sunflower seeds, rich in folate, good fats, and antioxidant Vitamin E, and Chia seeds, good in a smoothie or pudding, have almost eleven grams of fiber per ounce and are a great source of omega-3 oils and protein. Hemp seeds are another great choice, since they contain all nine essential amino acids and are considered a complete plant protein.

Green Heart Actions

- Unless you're allergic, add organic and salt-free nuts and seeds into your daily diet to reap their numerous health benefits.
- Buy packets of organic nut butters as a good way to "eat on the go." My favorite brand is Justin's.

Sugar and Spice and Everything Nice (and Not So Nice)

*My life is filled with sweet
things without adding sugar.*

As the general media have reported, too much sugar can rot your teeth, inflame your joints, damage the collagen and elastin in your skin, cause your liver to become resistant to insulin, damage your arteries, pancreas, and kidneys, and make you fat. What's tricky is that even when we think we're limiting our sugar intake—forgoing cakes, cookies, and candy—it's hiding out under names like fructose, corn syrup, and dextrose in many processed foods. As always, the best thing we can do is be informed consumers.

Artificial Sweeteners Are Not the Answer

Artificial sweeteners may sound like a good idea to add some sweetness without the calories, but I suggest you skip them. The most well-known artificial sweeteners include aspartame, which is sold under the brand names Equal and Nutrasweet; saccharin, sold as Sugar Twin and Sweet'N Low; and sucralose, which is sold as Splenda. The one thing they all have in common is that they are synthetic sugar substitutes and are not real food. You might think that since they are regulated by the FDA as food additives they must be safe; however, the FDA also has guidelines on what they consider to be an acceptable daily intake, indicating that too much may endanger your health.

According to a study done at Rockefeller University Hospital, artificial sweeteners can interfere with our metabolism, hinder the body's ability to process nutrients and regulate hormone responses, and cause changes in the gut's microbiome, which keeps blood sugar in check. Susan E. Swithers, a professor of behavioral neuroscience at Purdue University, has said, "We were once led to believe that 'light' and 'low tar' cigarettes are better choices than regular cigarettes; neither choice is actually healthy. It's time that we recognized the same thing about sweetened beverages."

Know the Facts About "Healthy" Sweeteners

Some might think that honey is a better alternative than sugar. While it does have a lower glycemic index than sugar—meaning it does not raise your blood sugar as quickly as sugar—it still affects your blood sugar, so it's not recommended for people with diabetes. Plus, teaspoon for teaspoon, it does have slightly more calories than sugar, so it's not going to help you watch your waist. As for the health of our planet, there are steps you can take to make sure that the honey you purchase is sustainable. Honeybees raised in large commercial operations, like other factory-farmed animals, can suffer from crowded and stressful living conditions. Also, some of the honey we find in our grocery stores is ultra filtered and may contain chemicals and antibiotics. And local is best. I always try to eat a teaspoon of local

---

Three Types of Stevia

GREEN LEAF STEVIA: This is what they've used in South America for centuries. The leaf is ground into a powder and is about thirty to forty times sweeter than sugar. In its pure form, it can fight cancers, improve cholesterol levels, lower blood pressure, and aid in weight loss.

STEVIA EXTRACTS: Some brands will extract the stevia and take away the bitter aftertaste, losing some of the health benefits along the way.

PROCESSED STEVIA: This is the one to avoid. The good stuff is extracted and replaced with chemical solvents and GMO additives.

---

honey the first day I travel to a new place as it helps acclimate me to that place. So my recommendation is to buy honey from local, small-scale producers at farmers' markets. You want to ask if they use natural beekeeping methods without chemicals.

Agave is another sweetener that has gained popularity recently. It is made from the sap of the blue agave plant, the same plant used to make tequila. Manufacturing agave requires the farmer to kill the plant completely, and the plants are not a quickly renewing resource. Agave is increasingly produced on large plantations that use chemical fertilizers, herbicides, and pesticides. The most sustainable options for agave are certified organic and free trade products.

Use Stevia as a Sugar Substitute

Stevia is arguably the best choice as far as sugar substitutes go. Stevia is an herb and has been used in Brazil and Paraguay as a noncaloric sweetener for more than 1,500 years. A stevia leaf used in its natural form will sweeten your tea without the calories, but when processed it requires quite a bit of water. If you must use a sweetener, use stevia and go online to find a source that is certified organic and Rainforest Alliance certified.

You Can Have Your Sweets and Eat Them, Too

Although my sweet tooth seems to have diminished, when I do need to be satisfied, I do one of two things: I reach for either a piece of fresh fruit or a high-quality dark chocolate with a cocoa content of more than 70 percent. Dark chocolate or cocoa consumed in moderation not only tastes great but also is fermented by gut bacteria into an anti-inflammatory compound that improves vascular function and cardiovascular health. The darker the chocolate, the less added sugar and fats.

Spice Is Nice

Spices enhance not only our cooking but also our health. Ginger is a great anti-inflammatory and is known to boost our immune system. Cumin can help fight infection and improve digestion. Turmeric contains the phytochemical curcumin, which may help inflammation. Paprika contains antioxidants, garlic has been linked to preventing heart disease and cancers, and cinnamon may help lower blood sugar. However, a key factor in getting the maximum health benefits from spice use is how the spice is harvested. Spices may become tainted when treated with chemicals in production. An FDA report in 2013 revealed that 12 percent of spices imported to the United States had been contaminated with insect parts, rodent hairs, and salmonella. Once again, the rule of thumb is to choose certified organic products.

Choose a High-Quality Extra-Virgin Olive Oil

Oil is an essential staple in the kitchen, both for cooking and flavor enhancement.

An extra-virgin, cold-pressed organic olive oil not only tastes the best but also is the healthiest for you. Studies consider it an essential part of a heart healthy diet, likely due to its high levels of monounsaturated fats and antioxidants. Unlike many commercial oils, this type of olive oil uses no chemicals in the extraction process. But keep in mind, you do not cook with olive oil. When used at high heat, it can produce carcinogens. Other oils such as canola, soybean, and corn have their own health issues that occur during growing or processing or in cooking. You also always want to stay clear of palm oil (unless it is organic red palm oil from a reputable brand like Nutiva). Palm oil is found in numerous products, so read your labels. Increased palm oil production can add to deforestation, loss of habitat for endangered species, and displacement of local communities in order to make room for palm plantations.

As we've seen, more traditional and slower methods of harvesting tend to use fewer chemicals and are less harmful to the environment. In the case of olive oil, cold-press expeller methods mean that the oil was mechanically extracted using a screw press. Big manufacturers avoid this because it takes longer, less oil is extracted, and the shelf life is shorter.

Go Beyond Extra-Virgin Olive Oil

There are other oils besides olive oil that are both good for you and the environment. Coconut oil contains medium-chain triglycerides, which can reduce cholesterol levels, and it's a great option, as long as it is organic and cold pressed. Like avocado oil, it is high in monounsaturated

---

Oil Brands to Look For

- California Olive Ranch
- McEvoy
- Newman's Own
- Nutiva
- Spectrum

---

fats and low in saturated fats and can be cooked at a high heat without breaking down. Coconut oil is frequently touted as a beneficial oil, and for good reasons. Coconut oil protects your body against free radicals, improves insulin secretion, promotes antiviral, antifungal, and antibacterial activity, and aids in cell regeneration.

Other oils that are generally good for you include hemp oil, extra-virgin sesame oil, walnut oil, and flaxseed oil. In all cases you want to look for organic, non-GMO, and cold-pressed labels to ensure that the oil was produced without harmful chemicals. Olive oil alternatives such as coconut and sunflower seed oils also are good for the water supply. To produce one pound of olives, it takes roughly 1,700 gallons of water, versus 800 gallons for one pound of sunflower seeds and only 500 for one pound of coconuts.

Be Careful of the Condiments

When I was growing up in Kentucky in the sixties, condiments were considered a food group.

At an early age, I got hooked on adding mayonnaise and ketchup to my burgers, soy sauce to my take-out Chinese food, and mustard and relish to my hot dogs. While I still add a little vegan mayo to my vegetarian burger these days, I am very careful about the type and amount of condiments I use.

By definition, a condiment is something used to enhance the flavor of food, which I am all for. In the case of processed condiments, it's not necessarily the condiment that is unhealthy but rather what it was made with and how much of it you use.

Most commercially prepared condiments, including mayonnaise and ketchup, are made with soybean oils and contain high-fructose corn syrups. A typical tablespoon of prepared ketchup contains four grams of sugar. Some brands use the label "natural flavoring," which is another way to disguise the use of MSG in the product. Read the label of a jar of most store-bought BBQ sauces and the first ingredient can be high-fructose corn syrup, followed by nothing that resembles real food. Bottled salad dressings are also full of additives, including food dyes and hydrogenated vegetable oils that are industrially processed and not the kind of oils and fats that are good for you.

I'm not suggesting that you will never get to taste mayonnaise again. What I am saying is that you should look for organic brands such as Organicville, Eden Organic, Primal Kitchen, or Woodstock Farms. Or you can make your own. Also keep in mind that condiments are not limited to prepared mustard and ketchup. They include

What MSG Does to Your Cells

MSG is short for monosodium glutamate. We think of MSG as a food additive typically used in Chinese food, but it hides out in many processed condiments under the heading of flavorings or seasonings. Including MSG in your diet on a regular basis overexcites your cells and causes damage that can range from headaches to brain damage and learning disabilities.

Katie's Cilantro Pesto

2 cups cilantro
¼ cup olive oil
¼ cup pine nuts
½ lemon, freshly squeezed
2 pinches of salt

Put into a food processor or blender for 30 seconds until smooth.

anything that will enhance the taste of your food. Consider a fresh pesto made with basil, olive oil, garlic, and pine nuts, homemade hummus, or guacamole. The most important thing to remember is that whatever your choice of condiment, it is made from real food.

Green Heart Actions

- Avoid all artificial sweeteners and refined sugars.
- When you need something sweet, go pure: a piece of fruit or a high-quality dark chocolate with at least 70 percent cocoa content.
- Use spices that are organically grown and free of pesticides.
- Choose 100 percent organic extra-virgin olive, coconut, avocado, sunflower, grapeseed, hemp, or other pure oils.
- Buy organic condiments that are free of artificial additives and preservatives or make your own.

Coffee and Tea

I am awake to the wonderful aroma of life.

Knowledge is one of the fastest routes to living with a green heart. The more you know, the better choices you will make for yourself and your family. One of the things I've discovered is that, very often, something I thought might be bad for me is better than I thought. Such is the case with coffee and teas. Both have good health benefits, and some even have medicinal properties.

Drink Responsibly

One of my friends cannot speak to anyone before she has a cup of coffee in the morning. She loves the aroma, the taste, and the jolt of caffeine to kick-start her day. Some might say this is an addiction, but she has one large cup in the morning and never after noon. She knows that although she craves it, she is sensitive to caffeine and more than one large cup will counteract her enjoyment of her morning java. She chooses to grind her own beans for freshness and to help prevent rancidity, and she always purchases coffee that is fair trade and shade grown. She uses a reusable filter so there is no extra waste, and if she does use filters, she chooses nonbleached ones to avoid those that use chemicals like chlorine in the bleaching process and may contain disinfection byproducts like dioxins.

Coffee, when enjoyed responsibly, is a great health elixir that has been proven through multiple studies to protect the heart and lower the risks of several cancers and Parkinson's disease. Recent research has also found that coffee contains an antioxidant compound that is well known for its antiviral, antiallergenic, antiplatelet, anti-inflammatory, and antitumor benefits. It can improve cognitive functions, and the flavonoids in coffee, such as hydrocinnamic acids and polyphenols, reduce the risks of heart disease, stroke, and type 2 diabetes, and protect against gallstones. All without a prescription from a doctor!

Do Decaf Right

Many believe that decaffeinated coffee or tea is decidedly better for you. That's definitely true if you're pregnant or if you're extremely sensitive to the effects of caffeine, but not otherwise. What you do want to pay attention to when choosing decaf beverages is the process used to take the caffeine out. Natural decaffeination uses ethyl acetate, which sounds like a harsh chemical but is a naturally occurring substance. CO_2 methods use CO_2 to decaffeinate. Swiss water-process methods use charcoal, but this process cannot be used for tea. Regardless of the process used, be aware that there is still some residual caffeine left in the beverage. What's important to check for is that no harmful chemicals are used in the decaffeinating process.

Recycle Your Coffee Grounds

Sprinkle them in your garden. Coffee grounds make excellent compost. Their acidity helps plants such as hydrangeas, azaleas, and rhododendrons bloom. Stirring a little into your watering can will give plants a nitrogen boost and help to aerate the soil. Also, keep a bowl of dried coffee grounds in the refrigerator or freezer to help absorb odors.

Read the Labels

Organic coffee is the **only** kind of coffee to buy. Coffee has traditionally thrived best when grown in the shade. The increased demand for coffee in the last forty years has led to modern methods of mass coffee production that include cutting down the shade canopies of trees, which contributes to deforestation and results in the loss of natural insect-killing birds. To compensate for this loss, pesticide use increased, making coffee one of the most highly pesticide-sprayed crops.

A Rainforest Alliance certification means that a particular coffee (or tea) is grown in a manner that protects those trees and meets the organization's standard for environmental, social, and economic sustainability. Also look for organic and fair trade certifications. This will

Look for the Green Frog

If it's certified by the Rainforest Alliance, a product will bear the official certified seal that shows a green frog, a symbol of environmental, social, and economic sustainability.

ensure that farmers were paid fair prices in decent living and working conditions and that the coffee and tea was grown sustainably.

Choose Organic, Sustainable Teas

I'm not sure when this habit started, but sometime in the past twenty years I started to drink Assam tea in the morning. I do drink coffee when I'm in a rush, but my preferred way to enjoy teas is to leisurely sip them while reading the paper (an e-paper), so this mostly occurs on weekends when life slows down.

Originally, much of our tea came from India, which was once under British rule, which may explain the enduring love of tea in England. As with other forms of agriculture, tea was traditionally grown in small amounts, but due to its growing popularity, it eventually became mass-produced. Pesticides were introduced to the crops to keep up with the demand, and in time, this industrial production model depleted the soil. As a result, local growers began to reemerge. They started "equal exchanges," where they can sell their teas to democratic alliances, and the alliances can sell to the tea brands to maintain fair trade standards.

Tea Brands That Promote Sustainability

- Numi
- Stash
- Traditional Medicinal
- Tazo
- Teeccino (a tea that is a delicious coffee substitute)
- The Republic of Tea

I would recommend that you look at all organically grown crops as a means to support small farmers and help families stay in business. This is particularly important in emerging countries, where a tea harvest may be the only thing that feeds a family for the year. When you are paying a premium for organic goods and services, it is a way of helping others make a living and care for their loved ones. It is the best way to care for the planet and its inhabitants, and it expresses your appreciation for the care that organic producers put into their craft. It's called gratitude, and it's a fundamental aspect of living with a green heart.

Green Heart Actions

- Choose USDA organic, fair trade, and Rainforest Alliance–certified teas and coffees.
- Other things to look for include shade grown coffees and coffees that are certified by Smithsonian Bird Friendly, Utz Certified, and the Non-GMO Project.

Alcoholic Beverages

I enjoy drinking responsibly.

There are many studies supporting the evidence that moderate drinking may be more beneficial than not drinking at all. Moderate drinking, defined as a glass of wine a day, has been shown to lower the risk of cardiovascular disease for both men and women, as well as reducing the risks of gallstones and type 2 diabetes. A glass of wine with a meal can also aid in digestion. However, any benefits are canceled out for heavy drinkers, and overconsumption of alcohol can cause disease, disrupt sleep, cloud judgment, and become addictive. I'm not advocating drinking; that is a personal decision. But if you do choose to responsibly enjoy wine, beer, or distilled spirits, you need to know what's in them and how they were produced.

Read the Label—but It's Not Enough

I have told you many times that the knowledge you gain from reading a book like this and checking ingredient labels is your best line of defense in living with a green heart. However, in the case of alcohol, the labels may not tell you everything you need to know.

The majority of the labeling requirements fall under the jurisdiction of the Alcohol and Tobacco Trade and Tax Bureau, which is part of the US Department of the Treasury. The exceptions are for beverages containing less than 7 percent alcohol, which are subject to FDA food labeling guidelines.

Liquor producers are required to issue a warning that too much alcohol may impair judgment. They must also say if their product contains sulfites—substances that may occur naturally or as a result of fermentation but can cause a physical reaction for someone who is highly allergic, like me. Winemakers generally tell where the wine was produced and which types of grapes were used, but unless a product is certified organic, you don't necessarily know how those grapes were grown or what additives may have been used.

Tito's Handmade Vodka's label tells you it is gluten-free and distilled six times and that it is "cleansed of phenols, esters, congeners and organic acids by filtering it through the finest activated carbon available," and also states that they are not required to provide this information. Diageo, which produces more than two hundred brands of spirits and beer, has voluntarily chosen to included caloric intake on its products, and many other brands are following suit.

Craft beers, many of which pride themselves on sourcing locally using sustainable methods, often include those features on their labels to promote their products. However, stating that a particular type of grain or fruit was used to make the beverage does not mean there were no pesticides or chemicals used in the production unless it specifically declares that to be the case.

Starting with the Soil

Regenerative agriculture is becoming more popular, and winemakers are leading the way. One of the largest and most successful wine producers in the world is the Jackson Family. Julia, daughter of founder Jess Jackson, is a friend of mine. She told me that the company is committed to increasing its green footprint. By 2021, 85 percent of their fruit will be from sustainable sources and 50 percent of all winemaking operations will be using onsite renewable energy generation. But Julia said it's really all about the soil. "[My father] had a knack for finding special sites and believing in the land's potential. He ingrained in me the idea of grapes expressing themselves through all the subtle nuances of microclimates, macroclimates and the concept of 'terroir' [the taste and flavor imparted to a wine by the environment in which it is produced]. While climate plays an extremely important role in how the grape expresses itself, equally important is the health of the soil. My family believes in regenerative farming practices. We've found a way to reduce chemical inputs and replace them by planting beneficial plants called 'cover crops' in between vineyard rows. These 'cover crops' are designed to sequester carbon [a process used to mitigate or defer global warming and avoid dangerous climate change] and attract beneficial insects, who then act to reduce the pest population. When we respect the land and its sanctity, it rewards us in beautiful ways."

Another Benefit of Organic Wine

Organic grapes used for winemaking contain an average 32 percent higher concentration of resveratrol, a phytonutrient that acts as an antioxidant, than conventional samples.

If You Are Going to Drink, Drink Sustainably

The carbon footprint varies among alcoholic beverages for wine, beer, and spirits—much of it resulting from transportation to the distributor. In other words, an organic or biodynamic wine can be grown sustainably yet may have a substantial carbon footprint, depending on how far it's shipped.

For spirits, distillation contributes the most to the carbon footprint, including the energy used in production and the wastewater and leftovers specific to the liquor distilled. The good news is that more and more distilleries are following the lead of breweries like New Belgium Brewing Company. New Belgium and its CEO, Kim Jordan, are well-known for their Fat Tire beer and their commitment to organics and climate change. New Belgium is the leader in using organic ingredients and renewable energies in their production processes.

Maker's Mark distills in small batches, buys local grains within a thirty-mile radius, and converts their waste into energy. Don Q Rum turns their waste into electricity and service water (which does not meet drinking standards but can be put to other uses), which they then sell to other businesses.

There is no doubt that biodynamic farming, small batch brewing, and sustainable methods may increase the price of your chosen libation, but they also make for a better-tasting and higher-quality product. And since drinking in moderation is key to the green heart approach, it doesn't have to cost more as long as you drink less.

Green Heart Actions

- Drink in moderation.
- Read labels and do research before you imbibe.
- Choose biodynamic and/or organic wines, spirits, or beer.

Nonalcoholic Beverages

I choose beverages that are good for me.

As a woman who is constantly on the go, I always try to leave home with a reusable water bottle made of glass or stainless steel tucked in my purse so I don't succumb to buying a single-serving plastic water bottle. However, like most of us, my world is not perfect and there are times when I find myself standing in front of a refrigerated case in an airport, determining which of my bottled options is the healthiest for me and will do the least damage to the environment.

Hydration is necessary for optimum health. Studies have shown that even mild dehydration can have an effect on physical performance, energy, mood levels, and brain function. There is no doubt that the best beverage for hydration is pure, clean water.

Unfortunately, water is not always what many of us reach for, especially when we are on the go. Data shows that of the $1,079.2 billion spent worldwide on nonalcoholic beverages, most of that is for carbonated soft drinks, and most of that for the full-calorie options. That is not good news from a health or an environmental standpoint.

Stay Away from Sugary Carbonated Beverages

In the case of sodas, sports drinks, and juices, the big health culprits are sugars and sugar substitutes. While there are debates about whether or not soda can really take the paint off of your car, studies have shown it will erode tooth enamel. For those living with a green heart, there is even more to consider than the amount of sugar in soft drinks, and it starts with the packaging.

We've already discussed the issues associated with plastic bottles, but it warrants saying again. Plastic is not good for you or the environment.

Aluminum cans, which reached a 56.7 percent recycling rate in 2014, are an improvement over plastic bottles. Aluminum recovered from recycling only requires 5 percent of the energy used in initial ex-

---

Eco-Friendly Reusable Water Bottles

- BKR
- EarthLust
- HydraFlask
- Klean Kanteen
- Kor
- Lifefactory
- S'well
- Welly

traction; however, the refining and smelting process to produce aluminum is a contributor to greenhouse gas emissions. Another thing to consider is the can lining. If the can is labeled BPA free, you know it's a better choice, but very few beverage cans have that designation (Spindrift uses a BPA free can, which is marked as such on their labels). And when the Center for Environmental Health tested seventy popular beverage cans, BPA showed up in all of them. I say, avoid cans altogether. Glass, which is made of sand and can be recycled, is a much healthier option; however, it can create a bigger carbon footprint because it is heavier and requires more fuel to transport.

The other thing to be aware of is carbonation. What makes carbonated drinks fizzy is carbon dioxide. When you pop open a soda can you are releasing a little carbon dioxide back into the air.

My best recommendation is to invest in an eco-friendly reusable water bottle and infuse that water with fresh fruit. It's much more

---

The Real Cost of That Cold-Pressed Juice (from the Modern Farmer)

Some people think cold-pressed juice is the healthiest option. It may offer health benefits for you, but it's not doing any favors for the environment.

- One hundred million 16-ounce servings of cold-pressed juice were sold domestically in 2015.
- A single 16-ounce serving of cold-pressed juice generates, on average, 3.5 pounds of pulp waste.
- The amount of pulp waste estimated to have wound up in landfills last year totals 175,000 tons.

The end result: the methane generated as the pulp decays emits CO_2 into the atmosphere.

economical and healthier. But, if you have to drink water on the go, look for newer packaging options such as Boxed Water or the plant-based plastics used in products like Just Water.

Green Heart Actions

- Avoid carbonated, sugary sodas, especially those in plastic bottles and cans.
- Organic drinks such as coconut water and kombucha can be enjoyed in moderation, but ultimately water is the best choice.
- Flavor your water with cucumbers, oranges, lemons, or limes.

HOME

---

*I treat myself, my home, and
my family with loving care.*

IN 1994, I WAS DATING A MAN whose house was literally falling down.
It would rain and he would look at me and say, "Hold on, we have
to put out the horse buckets, the roof leaks." How romantic . . . Having already been introduced to homeopathy and the health benefits
of leading a toxin-free life, I made a decision that the best way to start
my new life with this man was to rebuild his house and to do it as
green as possible. This was easier said than done because the world
of green building was not widely known at that time, and hence, I
began a journey of discovery into how I could protect myself and my
new family from the toxins in our home environment. That was
when I hired Mary Cordaro, the certified baubiologist, who came
with her team of environmental specialists to educate me on every-

thing I needed to know about building the safest, greenest, and most toxin-free home possible. As a life-long asthmatic, I was intensely interested in having the highest indoor air quality, and having just chelated mercury from my son's body, I wanted to have the cleanest water possible. But I learned much more, from toxin-free floor finishes and household cleaning products to designing a toxin-free bedroom. These and other tips are what I will share with you in the next sections.

Household Cleaning Products

---

*I use environmentally friendly
cleaning products in my home.*

Years ago, a housekeeper told me about a woman she had worked for who was so obsessed with cleanliness that she demanded the bathroom be cleaned with very strong chemical-based cleaning products, so she could smell the clean. No matter how many times she implored her to try less harmful options, she wouldn't listen. The woman was convinced nothing else would do the job.

This housekeeper needed the work, so she endured the toxic fumes these products emitted until one day, the off-gassing was so intense in the poorly ventilated bathroom that she literally passed out and hit her head on the toilet on the way down. Fortunately, she was not seriously injured, but the cost for a clean bathroom that day was a trip to the emergency room.

It may seem illogical, but as we try to keep our homes free of dust, allergens, and bacteria, if we do not choose our products carefully we may do more harm than good.

Beware of Hazardous Chemicals
You May Be Keeping Under Your Sink
or in the Laundry Room

Our obsession with cleanliness in this country is rooted in the early Puritan culture; however, it became costly during the post-WW2 industrial economic boom when advertisers, to sell new products and to build their business, convinced homemakers that old-fashioned methods of cleaning using baking soda and vinegar, which are still the most natural and most effective substances, were not enough. They needed to be replaced with easy, fast acting chemically based products. The part that never made it into the advertising copy was that while this might be an effective way to clean your bathtub or the kitchen floor, you would also be breathing in substances that might harm your health.

Cleaning product labeling in our country is as confusing as personal-care products This means it's up to you to choose consciously.

A study by the EWG found that 53 percent of conventional cleaning products can harm the lungs; 22 percent contained chemicals linked to asthma (www.ewg.org/guides/cleaners#.WyKhHxJKhE4). According to the American Lung Association, chemicals released when using cleaning supplies contribute to chronic respiratory problems, allergic reactions, and headaches. Studies are underway to assess how these chemicals affect people who have asthma and other respiratory illnesses. However, past studies indicate a link between chemicals from cleaning supplies and occupational asthma and other respiratory illnesses. Formaldehyde-releasing biocides may be present or be formed as a reaction to other ingredients when it hits the air. Products containing chlorine bleach may release chloroform, and many detergents contain 1,4-dioxane, which is believed to be a human carcinogen; bleach alternatives are just as harmful, so if you're going to use them, do so sparingly. And ingredients such as borax and boric acid, which

My Favorite Everyday Cleaning Products

- Arm & Hammer Baking Soda or Bon Ami Cleaning Powder
- Aspen Clean Natural Glass Cleaner
- Branch Basics Concentrate: Foaming Wash and Glass Cleaner
- Dot and Army Unpaper Towels
- Earth Friendly Products ECOS Dish Mate Dish Soap, Free & Clear
- Eco-Me Natural Plant Extracts Floor Cleaner with a Quick-Loop with a Shurline handle mop
- MamaSuds Automatic Dishwashing Powder
- Meliora Unscented Laundry Detergent and All-Purpose Cleaner
- Natural Value Walnut Scrubber Sponge or Trader Joe's Pop Up Sponges
- White or Apple Cider Vinegar

are added to cleaning products, may be hormone disrupters. The addition of quaternary ammonium compounds, fragrances, and artificial colors such as D&C violet 2 in fabric softeners and dryer sheets, poses dangers to the reproductive system and links to cancer. Antimicrobial or antibacterial ingredients are added to kill bacteria, viruses or molds. These biocides are usually listed as "active ingredients" and should be avoided. And what about inactive or inert ingredients? According to the EWG, there is no requirement to list them on the product label; only pesticides must be listed. "Inert" does not mean safe, but includes petroleum-derived solvents, preservatives or fragrances. EWG recommends that you choose products that list all ingredients whenever possible (www.ewg.org/guides/cleaners/content/decoding/labels). Off-gassing, the release of potential VOCs, is especially worrisome in indoor areas that are poorly ventilated, so use no or low VOCs in your products.

Labels to Look For

We're beginning to see transparency in ingredients happening at the state level. In 2017, New York became the first state to require manufacturers to disclose chemical ingredients in cleaning products with the establishment of the Household Cleaning Product Information Disclosure Program. California followed suit by signing the Cleaning Product Right to Know Act of 2017, requiring ingredients to be listed both on the product and online.

Some companies are following suit. SC Johnson is voluntarily disclosing possible allergens and offering information online at whatsinsideSCJohnson.com. Proctor and Gamble is planning full disclosure online by 2019.

Green Heart Actions

- Choose products that list all ingredients and avoid harmful chemicals.
- Skipping chemicals is best, but if you do insist on using products with them, make sure to store them properly, preferably outside in a storage shed. If you must keep them indoors, they should be in a box or bin away from your personal care products.
- Avoid fabric softeners and dryer sheets; a ½ cup of white vinegar will do in your rinse cycle.
- Try cutting back on your paper waste and see how long you can keep a roll of paper towels without replacing it.

The Family Room

I am at peace in my healthy home.

My grandmother's hobby was antiques. She, my Aunt Carie, and my Uncle Buck were in the antiques business, which had everything to do with the fact that the old 1812 farmhouse I grew up in was full of them. In fact, I don't remember my parents ever buying a new piece of furniture, except maybe mattresses or baby cribs. We simply traded pieces back and forth among the family when we moved or something didn't fit. At the time, it didn't occur to me that this recycling of furniture was an early precursor to me living with a green heart.

When it comes to furnishing your home, there are some things to look out for to protect your health and the health of the planet.

Say No to Flame Retardants

In 1975, California enacted a law known as Technical Bulletin 114, which required furniture manufacturers to treat their products with

---

Eco-Friendly Furniture Companies

- Urban Green Furniture
- EcoBalanza
- Pacific Rim

---

brominated flame-retardant chemicals in order to meet flammability standards. Not wanting to produce sofas and chairs for California any differently than for the rest of the country, national manufacturers began adding these chemicals to everything. Many nightwear manufacturers in the 1970s also started putting flame retardants in pajamas in case parents smoking in bed set the house on fire. I can clearly remember seeing the flame-retardant tag on my pajamas as a child.

At that time, no one was aware that these retardants, which used a chemical called trisphosphate, or tris for short, would be linked to endocrine and thyroid disruption, cancer, and neurological dysfunction, as well as adversely affecting fetal and child development. In 2009, the Centers for Disease Control and Prevention (CDC) estimated that Americans have three to ten times the levels of these toxic chemicals in their bloodstream than people from many European countries, where flame retardants are banned.

In 2014, California governor Jerry Brown signed a bill that required manufacturers to disclose if their products had a flame retardant. However, it is still not banned in the state. Thanks to the work of environmental scientist Arlene Blum and her team at the Green Science Policy Institute, things may be changing on a national level. In September 2017, the US Consumer Product Safety Commission published a notice in the *Federal Register* saying that these flame retardants present a serious health issue and should be banned. Despite the growing awareness, policy moves slowly, so there has been no law banning the use of the chemicals in the United States as of yet.

On a bright note, policy makers and administration leaders, at many enlightened universities, headed up by Heather Hendrickson and Jack Spengler at Harvard, have gotten together to create a "green buying group" that refuses to buy school furniture with flame retardants and other toxic glues. This is one step in keeping our children healthy and a huge step for these universities investing in the future of our planet.

Choose Natural Materials

Whether it's your sofa or dining room table, what your furniture is made of matters, both from a health standpoint and for the sustainability of the environment. Natural fibers, including organic cottons, down if you are not allergic, and wool are preferable, as are solid woods that do not contain or have low levels of glues, stains, varnishes, or laminations made with VOCs, which can cause respiratory problems.

The same holds true for window treatments, including drapes or shutters. Avoid blackout window treatments made with vinyl liners, polyester, azo-dyed fabrics, and any fabric that has been treated with

---

Eco-Friendly Window Treatment Brands

- Graber
- Hunter Douglas
- Plum Ridge (see their organic drapes)
- Pottery Barn (see their organic cotton drapes)

a chemical. Bamboo and pesticide-free hemp are eco-friendly choices in fabric. Also, even with eco-friendly materials, problems can arise with dust accumulation, so be sure to clean regularly.

Have a Really Clean Floor

As an asthmatic, I prefer hardwood floors or cork or linoleum that is made of all natural and biodegradable material rather than wall-to-wall carpeting, which can breed dust mites, mildew, and allergens. While this is my personal choice, whatever flooring you choose, it is important that you minimize toxic chemicals in your flooring, as they can be a source of indoor air pollution.

Vinyl floors, often made from reprocessed plastic, emit phthalates, lead, and flame retardants for the life of the product. Granite or other stones can emit radioactive elements such as uranium and thorium, which can contribute to lung cancer.

Solid hardwood is a good choice; you just need to be aware of its finish. Polyurethane gives a nice shine, but it is a petrochemical resin and known respiratory toxin. Water-based polyurethane is slightly better. If you do use it, one way to reduce the toxicity is to allow it to

---

Sustainable Carpet Brands to Look For

- Company C
- Earth Weave
- Flor
- Helios
- Shaw (look for the Cradle to Cradle certified organic ones)
- Woolshire

completely out gas—which could take anywhere from a few days to weeks—before you reenter your home. The best route to go is to use an environmentally friendly alternative such as linseed oil.

Carpeting, in particular wall-to-wall carpeting, might look nice, but it can be a significant contributor to indoor air pollution. Even with consistent cleaning and vacuuming, over time carpet will trap contaminates (heavy metals, pesticides, mold, dander, pollen). Many commercial carpets are produced with synthetic fibers, including vinyl, that have been made with PVC backings and treated with dyes, stain repellents, flame retardants, anti-microbial chemicals, and glues that emit VOCs.

William McDonough—architect, author, designer, innovator and friend—has recently released a new line of eco-friendly carpets in partnership with Shaw, using Cradle to Cradle design—an approach to design co-developed by McDonough, which is mindful of recyclability, renewable energy use, water efficiency and quality, and social responsibility. I had a chance to see one of his carpets laid out on an office floor and it was beautiful. Be on the lookout for more Cradle to Cradle Innovations designs in the future.

Whether you choose bare floors or carpeting, once again one of the most eco-friendly and sustainable choices available today is bamboo. It's natural, fast growing, free of VOCs, safe, and durable.

Green Heart Actions

- Choose furniture and window coverings that are made with natural fibers and are free of toxins such as flame retardants.
- Check wood furniture for mold.
- Choose solid hardwood floors, laminate flooring, tiling, vinyl, or linoleum that uses nontoxic glue and toxin-free finishes. Avoid formaldehyde.

- If you choose to use carpet, select one (and carpet pads) made of natural fibers that won't introduce VOCs such as benzene or SVOCs (semi-volatile organic compounds from flame retardants, azo dyes, or treatments that are anti-stain, anti-moisture, or antimicrobial) into the air.
- Keep your carpets clean by using an eco-friendly cleaning service.

The Bedroom

My bed is a place of well-being.

The bed is where we lay our heads to rest after a long day, exchange intimate moments with our partner, sleep to rejuvenate ourselves for our tomorrows, and spend almost a third of our life! We bring a lot to bed with us—the best and the worst of our day, our joys and our fears and our worries. Much of that we can't control, but what we can control is the environmental toxins we let in while in our restorative state.

Buy an Eco-Friendly Mattress

The average quality mattress lasts seven to ten years, yet most of us have not replaced ours in two decades or more. Beds can become a breeding ground for bacteria, causing mold and dust mites to grow, triggering allergies and asthma. Let's not forget to mention what an old, saggy mattress can do to the the health of our backs. Further, conventional mattresses are often made of petroleum-based petro-chemicals, plastics, flame-retardant chemicals, and synthetic latexes like styrene, a known human carcinogen. In combination they may release VOCs, which are linked to a host of problems from the obvi-ous respiratory illnesses to cancer.

I know that not everyone can afford to go out and buy a new mat-tress as a result of reading this book; however, when you do want to get a new mattress, you should look for an eco-friendly one. As the world of environmental goods has grown through the years, it now should be possible to find a green mattress within your budget.

Like all things in this book, I recommend that you look for a cer-tified organic mattress, but it might not be as easy as you think to find one without toxins. Years ago, mattress manufacturers started put-ting fire retardant in their materials to alleviate the risk of mattresses going up in flames from smoking in bed. Although the health dan-gers of these retardants have been demonstrated, mattress manufacturers have been slow to take them out. In fact, the Con-sumer Product Safety Commission still requires that mattresses meet flammability standards. Traditionally, this has meant that mattresses were treated with bromated or chlorinated flame retardants like chlo-rinated tris, which was the chemical that was removed from children's pajamas in the seventies when it was linked to cancer. In

---

Mattress Brands with Multiple Third-Party Organic Certifications

- Coco-Mat
- Naturepedic
- Savvy Rest
- Soaring Heart

2014, new anti-inflammatory standards were established in California as Technical Bulletin 11-2013 (TB117-201), and as before, other states have followed these standards. While they don't ban the use of the toxic chemicals, they do allow manufacturers to meet the requirements using safer options like wool or other batting. However, manufacturers have been slow to take out the chemicals because petrochemicals are cheaper than eco-friendly options.

When choosing an eco-friendly mattress you want to look for those made with untreated certified organic wool or Premium Eco Wool from the Woolgatherer Carding Mill, 100 percent natural latex, and organic cotton grown in pesticide-free soil. You also want to look for third-party certifications. A Global Organic Textile Standard (GOTS) certification means at least 95 percent of the mattress is made from certified organic materials. A Global Organic Latex Standard (GOLS) sets the same standard for latex. The Oeko-Tex Standard 100 does not require organic use, but it does limit VOC emissions and the use of toxic flame retardants and dyes. A Greenguard certification signifies that mattresses have been tested and have low levels of chemical emissions, Greenguard Gold being the highest award. They have more than forty-five thousand products listed in their database.

There are many organic mattress brands in the marketplace, but my favorite is Naturepedic. Naturepedic was founded by a man named Barry Cik, who was sent to the store by his wife to find a suitable baby mattress for their new grandchild. As an environmental engineer, he wanted to find the most eco-friendly mattress for this new beloved member of the family, but was appalled to find out that there were none available. So, he did what any proactive parent or grandparent would do and went out and started a mattress company. This was in 2003, when organic goods were just emerging on the horizon, so, in the beginning he only made baby mattresses. He contracted out the manufacturing part of the business and went door-to-door selling them himself, out of his garage. In a few years the babies had grown up, so he started making youth mattresses, and later this led to adult mattress sales. His success grew organically and was continued when his two sons, Jason and Jeff, joined the family business. Together they designed and built their own machines to make Naturepedic mattresses and set up production in a new facility in Chagrin Falls, Ohio.

Naturepedic has three types of mattress lines, depending on your budget. They are also test marketing an über-high-end mattress for those picky sleepers who want to count extra organic sheep at night. The interesting fact about Naturepedic's organic mattresses is that everything in them is organic. This means the wool comes from organic sheep, the latex is from organic sap trees, and the accessories are all Greenguard certified. I have slept on an organic mattress since 2004, and I can tell you that when I am not on it, I wake up with a stuffy nose. In addition, although not scientifically confirmed, studies show that dust mites have a less likely chance of hiding in natural latex or fabrics because these materials ventilate better, not allowing them to nestle into the fabric. Knowing my mattress is keeping dust mites away from me while I sleep allows me to sink into a deeper, more relaxed slumber.

Sleep on a Healthy Pillow

Because you lay your head, your face, your ears, your nose, and your mouth on the pillow, a healthy pillow is arguably more important than a mattress and less expensive, so, if nothing else, get yourself a eco-friendly pillow. A pillow should be made with organic material, so look for the organic label. It may cost more but it will be better for you.

Some hotel chains have figured out that pillows are important. Most business and upmarket hotels offer a pillow menu. Guests can choose

> ## Choosing the Right Pillow Is Like Choosing the Right Partner
>
> Depending on your personal pillow preferences, you might like firmer support, medium support, or little support. In all cases, you want a material that has not been chemically treated and is organic. Some materials to consider in your pillow:
>
> - Buckwheat
> - Kapok
> - Certified organic cotton
> - Certified organic wool or Premium Eco Wool from the Wool-gather Carding Mill

feather or foam or hypoallergenic batting. At some hotels, you can even request an eco-friendly room, with eco-friendly bedding and pillows. I love this idea, and although the hotel charges more for a room like this, it would be great if the ethical standards of people running hotels and motels were raised so that they would not invite guests to stay in rooms that contain toxic materials. The Joie de Vivre is a collection of hotels that are eco-friendly and I try to stay in one of their properties wherever I go. The Four Seasons is now working on eco-friendly rooms, as is Equinox. I applaud Hilton for making a commitment to corporate sustainability and for making it a priority in their hotels, and I am a regular Hilton guest because of it.

Don't Forget About the Mattress Pad

Choosing an eco-friendly mattress is just part of the greening of your bedroom. What you put on that bed matters, too. A mattress pad or cover not only protects your new mattress, it also can add fresh life to the one you already have. Protective mattress covers are your first line of defense from the dust mites and allergens that might be breeding in your mattress. You want to look for one that is completely nontoxic and made of organic and sustainable materials.

Sleep Wrapped in Green Comfort

Sheets are valued by their thread count because the higher the count, the softer the sheet. There is nothing worse than sleeping on a scratchy sheet and nothing better than sleeping on a soft well-worn one. Bed linens made with organic cotton are always your best choice as nonorganic material is heavily treated with pesticides during the growing process. Bamboo is a wonderful alternative, as it is a fast-renewing resource and therefore sustainable. It's a particularly good choice for sensitive skin because it is hypoallergenic, antimicrobial, and antibacterial. It also feels great. Personally, I'm an organic flannel sheet gal.

Another thing to keep in mind is how you wash your bedding. We've already discussed the importance of using toxin-free detergents in the chapter on cleaning products, but it warrants mentioning again. The greenest sheets are only as good as what you wash them with.

Beyond the Bed

Now that you've ensured that what you're sleeping on is eco-friendly, think back to the early sections of the book on the air we breathe and EMFs. Both affect the quality of your sleep and therefore your health. We can't always control them during our days when we're out and about, but if there is one place we do have a say, it is in our bedroom.

Buy a HEPA or carbon filter for cleaner air in the bedroom and please leave electronics outside the bedroom. Although the HEPA or carbon filter runs on electricity, if it is the only thing in the room that is running, its benefit outweighs its hazard. Just make sure it's at least three feet from your head and preferably across the room. If you live in a neighborhood with no cars driving by all night, the best choice is to open the window and enjoy the breeze.

Protect the Quality of Your Sleep

The quality of sleep has everything to do with what's in your mind and in your heart when you go to bed. If you had a bad day, you may be hashing out all the ways you could have done things differently. Or if you left too many things undone, how you plan to get them done tomorrow. Or maybe you feel emotionally wounded by a verbal or physical exchange you're mulling over. As this is a book about how to lead a more personally environmentally friendly life, I will offer a few psychological tips that I use that may be helpful in your own journey. Sleep is one of the traditional pillars of good health, so it is critical that you honor your and others' need to sleep, as it recharges your physical and mental batteries. If in doubt about how important sleep is to your well-being, read Arianna Huffington's book, *Thrive*, where she discusses the health benefits and says "Everything you do, you'll do better with a good night's sleep."

One thing I recommend is following a bedtime ritual. As silly as it sounds, I follow the same routine that I have followed since I was a child. First, I make a cup of tea adding in a few drops of Bach Flower Remedies. Then I tidy up my room or the house, organizing it for maximum efficiency when I get up the next morning. When my kids were little, this meant getting their lunch boxes ready, laying out their clothes, setting the breakfast table, and making lists. Now, this

Tips To "Feng Shui" Your Bedroom

Feng shui is the ancient Chinese art and science of arranging space to have favorable energy flow. Feng shui practitioners believe how you arrange your bedroom can determine how peacefully you sleep. I have been consulting with one, Ginger Lai, for over twenty years and believe feng shui makes good common sense.

- Place your bed against a wall where you can see the door, but not in a direct line with it.
- Do not store boxes and papers underneath your bed.
- Keep your bedroom free of electronics, including TVs, computers, and smartphones.
- If you have a mirror, do not place it facing the bed.
- Do not put the head of your bed on a wall that adjoins the bathroom, as it will promote colds.

mostly means finding things I need that have been misplaced (like my reading glasses), plugging in my computer, getting the coffee maker ready and taking the dog out. Moving into personal care, I brush and floss my teeth, wash my face, and perform other nightly beauty rituals (which are getting more extensive with age). Once I am in bed, I read until drowsy (sometimes this is less than five minutes). After I close my eyes, I say prayers, count my blessings and then it's lights out. It is important to note here that I have a very strict policy of only glancing at my phone after dinner to answer time sensitive texts from friends or family, and rarely, if ever, sitting at my computer at night. I like having device-free evenings so that I can savor that quality time with myself or loved ones.

You might wonder why I'm getting into this level of detail about my daily process. I am hopeful that by hearing mine, you might look at your own habits and be aware of what you do and what you could do differently. I believe it is good environmental hygiene to take care of your body, your mind, and your spirit before heading off to the Land of Nod, and l encourage you to create your own ritual that will work best for you.

Green Heart Actions

- Choose an organic, and eco-friendly mattresses and bedding made with materials such as organic cotton or bamboo.
- No cell phones in the bedroom.
- Create a bedtime ritual that promotes restful deep sleep.

The Kitchen

The kitchen is the healthy heart of our home.

Although it was unusual in the 1960s, both of my parents worked outside the home. Still, we somehow managed to sit down in the kitchen at 6:30 P.M. every night and eat dinner as a family. The kitchen was the center of our home, a place to prepare and cook food, provide nourishment, and exchange conversation. While the tradition of the daily "family dinner" seems to have gone out of style, cooking healthy meals that are free of harmful chemicals has not. I've devoted a lot of time in this book to the food you choose, and now I want to talk about how you cook it.

Say No to Teflon

After reading this far, it will come as no surprise that anything treated with chemicals is not good for you. That includes pans and utensils that are promoted as nonstick and easy to clean because they have been coated with materials like Teflon.

Teflon contains chemicals which fall under the heading of perfluorinated compounds (PFAS). PTFE (polytetrafluorethylene) is a chemical that has been around since the 1940s, because of its frictionless (nonstick) stable surface properties. PFOA (perfluorooctanoic acid) is an ingredient that is used in the process of making Teflon, and although it is burned off during the process, it is a real health concern because it can stay in you or the environment for a very long time. The American Cancer Society estimates it to be in the bloodstream of almost all Americans and in our drinking water. PFAS have been linked to cancers of the liver, testicles, mammary glands, and pancreas as well as thyroid imbalances, weakened immune systems, and low-weight births. What is even worse is that when nonstick cookware containing PFAS, as well as those made with silicon, are used at high heats, they off-gas and release toxins into the air. The EWG has found that the breakdown can occur at heating levels as low as 325 degrees Fahrenheit (www.ewg.org/research/canaries-kitchen/teflon-off-gas-studies).

Another problem with nonstick cookware is that you need to be careful what utensils you use so as not to nick through the treated surface. Plastic utensils are often recommended, but the plastic can leach into your food when heated.

The good news is that due to the work of the EWG, PFOA—the chemical used to make the PTFE in Teflon is being phased out. What you want to be aware of is that other chemicals are being introduced to create nonstick surfaces. Their safety has yet to be determined, but my inclination is always to avoid anything that has been chemically treated; so stay away from Teflon. Its convenience does not outweigh its hazards.

Invest in Eco-Friendly Cookware

Investing in good cookware and utensils that are not treated has several benefits. Not only will your cooking be healthier, your food will also cook more evenly and taste better. Lastly, unlike the cheaper, often chemically treated options, the investment can last a lifetime.

One popular option is stainless steel. My only caution is that most brands are made of a combination of metals, often including nickel, so if you have a sensitivity to that metal you want to read the fine print. I use the brands All Clad and Le Creuset (enameled cast iron) and good old cast iron black frying pans from the hardware store.

Cast iron, once seasoned, is naturally nonstick, easy to use, and easy to clean. And these pans last so long you might have to put them in your will. Cast iron will give off trace amounts of iron when you cook; unless you have a health issue that requires you watch your iron intake, this can be an extra benefit.

Glass and ceramics are also clean and eco-friendly choices for cookware; just make sure these pieces aren't treated with any toxic glaze.

Wood cooking utensils are always preferable to plastic ones, and they can last for years. They're also good to use on the nonstick pans you can't yet let go of as they will not scratch the surface. It's important to keep them clean, as they can breed germs. (This goes for your wooden cutting boards, too.) But don't put wood in the dishwasher as it will dry out. I like to dry my cutting boards in the sun.

Think About Getting Rid of Your Microwave

Like many, I have always used a microwave for convenience, but the health risks associated with microwave use just aren't worth it.

Microwave Safety Tips

- Always transfer food to glass or ceramic containers labeled for use in microwave ovens.
- If you must cover your dish in the microwave, use kitchen parchment paper, cloth or dampened paper towels.
- Many takeout containers and (all) plastic tubs or jars made to hold margarine, yogurt, whipped topping, etc., are NOT microwave safe.
- Old, scratched, or cracked containers, or those that have been microwaved many times, may leach out more plasticizers, chemicals added to a substance to make it flexible. Please recycle these.
- Styrofoam is subjected to the same rules as other plastics when it comes to the microwave. Avoid Styrofoam in general.

First off, microwaving food strips away its nutrients. Microwaved food loses about 30 percent to 40 percent of its nutrients, and the heating process negates any of the vitamin B_{12} that the food originally contained.

Even more concerning than the loss of vitamins are the health risks associated with microwaving. In one Swiss clinical study, researchers note changes in the blood of participants who consumed microwaved milk and vegetables. The results of the study showed that levels of red blood cells decreased while white cell levels increased, along with cholesterol levels. The nonionizing radiation of the microwave can also cause changes in your heart rate. A study conducted by the botanist Magda Havas, Ph.D., of Trent University found that the levels of radiation emitted by a microwave affect both heart rate and heart rate variability. These levels are

Microwave Safety

By keeping at least three feet from your microwave while heating up food, you can keep harmful EMFs from coming into contact with your body. Although a minute here and a minute there seem like small amounts of time, bio-accumulation adds up.

within federal safety guidelines but tend to cause immediate and dramatic changes in heart rates. If you experience an irregular heartbeat or any chest pain and regularly eat microwaved food, your microwave may be the culprit.

If you do insist on microwaving food, please, please, please do not use plastic. When the food heats up in a microwave, the plastic also heats up and melts, which means that there might be a little bit of plastic that leaks into the food and the air around the food each time you microwave something. Plastic wrap heated in the microwave has been found to release carcinogens along with other harmful toxins into your food. Just keep all plastic out of the microwave.

Should You Cook with Gas or Electricity?

There is not an easy answer to this question. The US Department of Energy estimates that less than 4.5 percent of an average household's energy use comes from cooking, which may be the reason these are the one set of appliances that there is no Energy Star standard for.

Overall, gas ranges can be considered more energy efficient since generating the electricity for an electric range uses more energy. However, only 6 percent of the energy in a gas stove goes directly to cooking food, while in using an electric stove, 12 percent to 14 percent does. Newer induction ovens create heat faster, which is an advantage when cooking and from an energy use standpoint.

When it comes to stoves, you also may be limited by your energy source. If you don't have a gas line in your home, you may be forced to go electric. If so, do not purchase an induction stove which emits extremely high levels of EMFs. Purchase a traditional, thermally based cooktop without an induction feature. In any case, as always, do your research and find the stove that is right for you. Whichever you choose, it is important to have a hood fan over the stove that works properly and is always on when cooking; both gas and electric stoves emit high levels of pollutants when cooking.

Choose the Most Energy-Efficient Appliances

One of the many things I learned from my maternal grandmother was what she called the proper way to hang one's laundry outside on a clothesline. She believed you could tell a lot about a woman by the way she hung out her clothes and sheets. It might sound archaic today, but my grandmother grew up at a time when a chore like this was considered to be reflective of a woman's character. Since most women were not allowed to work outside the home, their self-esteem and status were tied up with how they kept their children and their home.

In today's world, where we're all about speed and efficiency, it's rare to see anyone dry clothes outside. And while I'm not suggesting that you forego your dryer and hang a clothesline in your backyard, if you really want your sheets to get that fresh-air smell, it's a great idea. Nor will I tell you to skip the washing machine, the dishwasher, or—heaven forbid—the coffee maker. But there are tips you should know so you can choose energy-efficient appliances, reduce electric costs, and thus minimize the emissions released from our high consumption of electricity.

Pay Attention to the Energy Star Label

Energy Star certification is backed by the US government and is based on a set of criteria that were established to help reduce greenhouse gas emissions and make it easier for us as consumers to identify the most efficient energy choices on the market. Appliances bearing this label use at least 20 percent less energy than the federal standards and meet current EPA guidelines. It's not just about electricity. A report that was published in 2012 by David Korn and Lauren Mattison of the Cadmus Group, Inc. compared a base of twenty-four non–Energy Star washers with ninety-one that were Energy Star certified. The difference in energy use was not significant, however, the savings was in the water usage, with Energy Star machines using 55 percent less water. Always look for the Energy Star label.

Just Because You Turned It Off, That Doesn't Mean It's Off

The good news is that we're producing more energy-efficient appliances than ever before. The bad news is that there are more of them, and because of technology and the evolution of smart appliances that are always on and connected to the Internet, we're using more electricity and—as we discussed at the beginning of the book—emitting more harmful EMFs than ever before. Even the digital display on an appliance that has been turned off continues to draw energy.

The idea of "unplugging" has come to be associated with turning off the technology, having a Zen moment, and listening to your breath—which I am all for. However, there's also a benefit to literally unplugging your devices. In addition to reducing EMFs, you'll also save electricity. When you leave an appliance like a coffee maker plugged in, even when it is not in use, it's drawing what is called

The Power of a Power Strip

An easy and inexpensive way to cut back on energy use is to use a power strip for multiple appliances, allowing you to turn them all off at the same time.

MY FAVORITE EVERYDAY KITCHEN PRODUCTS

- Bamboo cutting boards and cooking tools
- Duralex food storage containers
- Etee reusable food wraps and beeswax wraps from Bee's Wrap
- Litter Free Lunch Box Kit from Thrive Market or the Tri Bento from Eco Lunch Boxes
- Reusable glass coffee cup (I like the JOCO brand)
- Stainless steel straws from Dot and Army, or glass ones from Simply Straws
- Stasher reusable silicone food storage bags
- Weck jars and Mason jars
- Zero Waste Utensil Wrap from Dot and Army

phantom power. It's estimated that the average household has forty such appliances that contribute to 10 percent of household energy use. And according to the US Energy Information Administration, approximately 37 percent of all CO_2 emissions in the United States came from electricity production in 2016. Every little green heart action you can take, including unplugging the toaster oven, will help to collectively make a difference.

Green Heart Actions

- Avoid all Teflon and all nonstick coatings in cookware and utensils.

- Choose cookware that is made with high-quality stainless steel, or cast iron.
- Choose utensils that are made of bamboo or solid wood and stay away from plastic or silicon.
- Buy Energy Star–certified appliances.
- Find a way to power down your kitchen appliances at night to conserve energy.
- Unplug countertop appliances when they are not in use.
- Never use plastic in the microwave. Try using cloth towels to avoid paper.
- Find a way to replace those disposable baggies with eco-friendly reusable ones or use glass storage containers.

The Bathroom

I let life flow freely without fear.

It may be the smallest room in the house, but we spend a lot of time in the bathroom, and without proper ventilation, water-saving measures, and choosing the right products, it can be a haven for toxins, off-gassing, mold, and mildew.

Save Water and Money

One of the easiest ways to green your bathroom is by monitoring water consumption. Between showering, brushing our teeth, and using the toilet, the greatest percentage of all indoor water use comes from the bathroom.

The average family uses close to forty gallons of water a day for showering. Older toilets can use up to seven gallons of water with every flush and with an average of five flushes a day, using up to

12,000 gallons a year compared with newer high-efficiency WaterSense-labeled toilets, which use 1.6 gallons of water per flush, reducing water waste to around 2,900 gallons per year

Checking for leaky toilets and repairing them, replacing them with low-flow options, and installing atomizing showerheads that use 70 percent less water may sound like an expense at first, but not only are you conserving water, you're also saving more money in the long run by lowering your water bill

Install an Efficient Showerhead That Has a Filter

If you don't have a filtration system in your home, choose a showerhead that is both water efficient and a filter. Like the water we drink, we want to be sure the water we bathe in is clean, so that we don't absorb toxins like chlorine through our skin.

Keep the Bathroom Dry

Keeping the bathroom dry can be a challenge, given all that showering and washing, but it is necessary. Mold and mildew can thrive in moist environments with little or no ventilation and can cause a variety of health issues, including upper respiratory illness and asthma. A few simple things you can do include picking up damp towels off the floor and drying them out immediately, wiping down the tiles in the shower after use, and, if you don't have the benefit of an exterior window in your bathroom or can't open the window in cold weather, making sure you have some sort of extractor fan installed to pull moist air out.

Shower curtains can be another place where mold and mildew are likely to grow if they're not wiped down frequently. Those made

---

Check Your Shower's Flow Rate

- Place a bucket that measures gallons under your showerhead.
- Turn on the shower.
- Time the number of seconds until the water in the bucket reaches the one gallon mark.
- Anything less than twenty seconds means you are using more than 3 gallons per minute. According to government standards, it should be no greater than 2.5 gallons per minute.

---

with PVC are especially hazardous as they are prone to off-gassing. The solution is to choose PVC-free curtains or hemp curtains when possible as hemp is naturally resistant to mold.

What you put on the bathroom floor can also curtail mold and mildew. While synthetic choices in bathroom carpeting are plusher and softer to your bare feet than those made of organic cotton or bamboo, they are also deceptively good at attracting mold and mildew, despite the number of times that you wash them in nontoxic detergent. Above all, never lay down wall-to-wall carpeting in a bathroom. It traps the mold and mildew underneath and is almost impossible to dry out completely.

If You Can Choose Your Tub . . .

We aren't all lucky enough to be able to remodel our bathroom and choose the materials our bathtubs are made of, but when you have that luxury, choose materials that are environmentally friendly. Stainless steel tubs are less likely to leach toxins; just be sure the tub has a ceramic or porcelain finish that is lead free. Cast iron tubs, while quite heavy, are also unlikely to leach toxins and have the added benefit of keeping the water warmer, which can lower your heating costs. Fiberglass is affordable, but there will be some off-gassing that can last anywhere from three months to a few years.

Even when you're not remodeling, make sure to keep everything sealed and, when re-caulking, to choose grouts that are chemical free.

Green Heart Actions

- Choose water-saving toilets, sinks, and showers, such as a low-flush toilet and aerated faucets. Use food coloring to check for a leaky toilet. Place ten drops in your toilet tank, close the lid and do not flush. Wait about ten minutes. Then check the water in your bowl; if it is colored you have a leaky toilet.
- When choosing a tub, consider options that are environmentally friendly and less likely to leach harmful chemicals, such as stainless steel, cast iron, wood, or ceramics, avoiding fiberglass and plastic tubs.
- If you opt for a porcelain or enamel coating, make sure it is lead free.
- If creating a tub or shower surround, look for natural materials such as plaster.
- Clean your bathroom with eco-friendly supplies.
- Find a way to properly ventilate your bathroom and run an extractor fan for two hours after showering.

The Garage

I treat every part of my home with care.

Aside from getting in and out of my car, the garage is the only place in my home that I don't frequent often. My son Alex, on the other hand, loves to spend hours there tinkering with his tools and organizing camping gear. There is no one I know who better understands what's important to greening a garage than him, which is why I decided to ask him to help me write this chapter.

As he pointed out to me, the garage is often overlooked when it comes to greening our lives. While we think the garage's primary purpose is to house our cars, many of us also use it to store machinery, recreational equipment, maintenance items, and those things we don't know where else to put. It's a room that, if we're not careful, can be a breeding ground for contaminants. Alex offered these steps to keep your garage as green and environmentally friendly as possible.

Seal Your Floor

Most garages have a concrete floor, which is naturally porous and can easily absorb fluids that might leak from your automobile. Applying an epoxy seal to the floor can minimize this.

Keep It Ventilated

Installing a good ventilation system will help to create a fresh airflow and allow noxious fumes from the engine of your car to dissipate.

Check for Leaks from Your Car's Engine

Use a leak pan to catch any known (or unknown) leaks from your car or truck. This will catch fluids that can then be disposed of in an environmentally safe way.

Insulate the Garage Door and Walls

A lot of the heat in your home is lost through the garage. Checking for and repairing cracks, as well as installing environmentally friendly insulation, can minimize that loss and reduce your carbon footprint. This can also keep your garage pest free and stop those pests from entering your home.

There is no Energy Star–approved garage door, but there are doors that contain eco-friendly insulation and are more environmentally friendly than others.

The Crawl Space

Bill Hayward, founder of the Hayward Score, a company to help home owners assess the health of their home, says, "Studies have shown that up to 40 percent of the air in the home comes through the crawl space. This means that moisture, mold, dust, and pathogens are effectively entering your home. For crawl spaces with unsealed dirt floors, there can be a risk of radon exposure." Make sure to have these areas properly sealed and ventilated.

Store Responsibly

The garage is often the place we store the things we don't want in the house. That often includes old paints, antifreeze, or lawn mower oil. My hope is that you are choosing the greenest and least toxic brands, but in any case, Alex suggests purchasing a locked and sealed metal storage locker to keep these chemicals as contained as possible.

For home goods that you're storing in the garage, BPA-free plastic bins can limit contamination at the same time as they will keep

---

Toxins Commonly Found in Garages

- Ammonia
- Benzene from gasoline
- Ethylene glycol from antifreeze
- Ethylene glycol monobutyl acetate from paints and solvents
- Hydrofluoric acid from aluminum cleaner
- Oil and gasoline
- Sodium hypochlorite
- Toluene from paint

those treasured Christmas decorations and old pictures safe from any pests, roof leaks, and other toxins that sneak through your preventive measures.

Often that old refrigerator you can't part with winds up in the garage and becomes a place to store extra beverages. Older models were not made as sustainably and often contain Freon, the registered patent name for DuPont's dichlorodifluoromethane (a type of CFC) and hydrochlorofluorocarbon (HCFC) refrigerants. In addition to being linked to respiratory illness and organ damage, Freon is now considered a cause of ozone depletion.

Reuse and Recycle

Our garage has always been the dumping ground for old sports equipment and discarded hobbies, so we choose a day once or twice a year to have a family clean-out day. It's amazing what you can find if you start to clean up together. This a great green heart family activity. You may decide to donate or sell items you no longer use, or you may rediscover an old passion.

Green Heart Actions

- Avoid storing toxic chemicals in your garage.
- Keep the garage well ventilated, especially if it connects to your home. Make sure the door that connects to the garage and your home closes tightly.
- Keep your garage free of clutter.
- Keep the floor sealed.
- Watch for car leaks.

Waste Disposal

I only buy things I need.

In 1969, after the oil spill in Santa Barbara, a few concerned citizens got together and held an environmental rights conference at Santa Barbara City College. Some of those who attended went on to write a pamphlet called *Everyman's Guide to Conservational Living*, which I discovered one day when browsing in my local bookstore. Mary Sheldon, the store manager, was one of the concerned citizens who co-authored the book, and after a few weeks of me stalking her, she gave me a copy of the original pamphlet. It was one of the inspirations for this book.

The first thing that struck me as I started reading it was that not much had changed. The first sentence in the book reads, "The need for action has become clear. For many, however, the question 'What can I, as an individual, do?' is still unanswered."

The focus of the pamphlet was "consumption," and in the opening, the writers gave numerous examples of overconsumption and offered concrete steps that citizens of Santa Barbara County could take on a personal level to cut down on their clutter and its resulting environmental footprint. In most instances, the authors suggested basic actions and local places where people could go to get help.

What I found so interesting is that their General Rules to Live By still hold up today.

1. Don't use more than you absolutely need to survive.
2. Eliminate the "I want" philosophy of life.
3. "Eat to Live, Don't Live to Eat."
4. Don't buy more than you need . . . fight needless consumption.
5. Buy long-lasting items, not those designed for obsolescence.
6. Make what you can, bake what you can, grow what you can, avoid what you can.
7. Alert yourself and others to the overt despoilers of the world, then support any political (or nonpolitical) action (or inaction) that tends to alleviate the problem.
8. Fight the social myths: "growth," "progress," "development." Natural growth and development are much more beautiful.
9. Fight the social pressures for baby production and large families.
10. Set a good example yourself of what you think the concerned person should exemplify in terms of living style, awareness, waste, consumption, reproduction and informing others.

Everything that was said in this pamphlet is still true almost fifty years later. Our world had not heeded these words of the

The Truth About Trash

- We generate close to 270 million tons of waste in the United States each year. That equals 4.5 pounds of waste per person per day.
- Here in the U.S. we produce more waste than any other country in the world.
- The majority of waste generated is made of paper, paperboard, metals and plastics; the vast majority of this material can and should be recycled. Another 15 percent is made up of food waste and 13 percent is green waste, both of which can be composted.
- Fifty-five percent of all waste gets buried in landfills, only 33 percent gets recycled and 12.5 percent goes to incinerators.
- China, which has been taking over 60 percent of the recycled material generated in the U.S., is now refusing to accept any more because of the amount of contaminants.
- Plastic waste is one of many types of wastes that take too long to decompose. Normally, plastic items can take up to one thousand years to decompose in landfills.

early activists, and as a result, we've ended up with mountains of trash.

This pamphlet came to mind when I was talking to my friend, Dave Aardsma, who is the Chief Sales and Marketing Officer of the largest waste and recycling company in the United States, Waste Management Inc. He was sharing with me some of the statistics about how big an issue waste is here in our country and around the world. We are such a wasteful society, which is probably due to the fact that our waste gets picked up so efficiently every week. Here are some of the facts from Dave.

Clear Out the Clutter

Clutter is really a form of pollution. It pollutes your mind and your home. Piles of unnecessary things collect dust, resulting in poor air quality and an increased risk of allergens or asthma attacks. Clutter also pollutes your mind by making your home less organized, adding stress and guilt. Clutter is the result of overconsumption, and it pollutes our planet by ending up in crowded landfills. If you need to be convinced not to buy more stuff, watch the *Story of Stuff* or read one of my favorite books by Marie Kondo, *The Life-Changing Magic of Tidying Up*; it will cure you from ever wanting to shop again.

Health benefits to decluttering your home include reducing anxiety and stress, improving sleep, ridding your home of allergens, taking control of your spending, and increasing productivity.

If you have allowed clutter to build up in your home, don't lose heart! While it may seem a daunting task to clear it, remember that it didn't accumulate in a day and it won't be resolved immediately, either. Tackle the problem room by room. Seeing a result in one space will inspire you to keep going.

Things to recycle immediately: old bills, receipts, and tax documents more than three years old. You don't even need to keep physical copies of anything. Scan any important documents and store them digitally. Appliance manuals can usually be found on the Internet, so you can get rid of those. Toss expired beauty products. Even cosmetics have a shelf life, and it's not healthy to use old products where bacteria may be growing. Some beauty brands such as Aveda, Lush, and MAC will recycle your empty or old products and will even reward you for your green efforts. Get rid of old clothes. My rule of thumb is, if I haven't worn it in a full year, I probably don't need it anymore. Get rid of anything that no longer fits you or your lifestyle. Donate what you can and recycle the rest if your community has a fabric-recycling program. If you have gently used business clothes, consider donating them to Dress for Success.

Don't use your newfound space to buy a lot more stuff! Enjoy the cleanliness and order of your home, and I assure you, it will help your mind!

Green Heart Actions

- Educate yourself to ensure you are recycling the right material. Rules can vary from city to city.
- Create a well-organized waste-removal system, including food scrap composting and glass, aluminum, plastic, and paper recycling bins.
- If you are inclined, learn to compost. It will help your lawn and garden. By spreading your own compost, you will be adding organic matter, water-holding capacity, and nutrients to your soil for a healthier crop. It also saves on having to purchase fertilizers. You can also grass cycle your lawn clippings. This is a simple process of allowing the cut blades to fall on the lawn instead of being collected and hauled away. Not only will they provide a valuable source of nitrogen, it will help retain moisture in the soil.
- Before you throw anything out, see if you can find it a new home, a second life.
- Before you buy anything new, ask yourself if you really need it.
- Join Terracycle. Sign up your home, school, or office to recycle bottles and cans; they reward you for recycling everything!

LIFESTYLE

Pets

I care for all living creatures.

Having cared for pets for most of my life, I understand entirely the close bond that forms between humans and their animal companions. I am as guilty as anyone of spoiling them in return for their unconditional love.

The majority of Americans have at least one pet, and of those pet owners, close to three quarters have at least one dog and nearly half have cats. According to a Nielsen survey, 95 percent of pet owners consider their pets to be a part of the family.

It's no surprise, then, that the same steps we are taking to improve our health and that of our loved ones are being extended to our furry family.

Pets bring joy to our lives and have been shown to improve our health by decreasing blood pressure, lessening anxiety, and boosting immune systems. The *Harvard Medical Journal* reports that having a dog may lower the risk of heart disease, in part by making us more active but also through companionship. Unfortunately, despite all of the benefits that pets bestow, they are having a significant negative environmental impact, just like their humans. That impact is mostly attributed to the fact that our more than 160 million cats and dogs are meat eaters and because their waste is difficult to manage.

As pet lovers and environmentalists, this poses a dilemma. While we want our pets to be as happy and healthy as possible, we also understand that we need to be as concerned about their carbon "paw prints" as we are about our footprints. We are increasingly seeking out products and care that are good for our pets, good for our human family members, and good for the Earth and its creatures. How we treat our pets, feed them, and clean up after them has a sizable impact on the environment.

As I said earlier in the book, living with a green heart is a personal journey. This chapter delves into factors to consider while balancing your pet's well-being with your commitment to the environment. I have focused on cats and dogs since they are our most common pets and have the most significant environmental impact, but many of these issues can be thought starters for other types of pets as well. These are options for you to consider incorporating into—or eliminating from—your pet's feeding, grooming, and waste removal practices, to design the perfect green heart plan for you and your entire family.

Is Organic the Right Food Choice for Your Pet?

For those of us who have committed to eating organic to improve our health and protect the Earth, it seems like a natural conclusion that we would want our pets to share in the same benefits. Fortunately, organic pet food—like organic human food—has become more common in the past few years and is much easier to find at our local grocery and pet stores—or online—than ever before, and at more affordable prices.

If you do go organic with your pet's diet, some of the health benefits you may expect to see include fewer allergies and digestive disorders, better weight management (organic food is more nutrient dense, so your pet will need to eat less), and stronger immunity. According to the International Boarding & Pet Services Association, better nutrition provides an overall boost in the immune system and improved health over the long term with less stress on the pet's organs. The kidneys and liver have to work very hard to remove toxins such as chemicals, preservatives, dyes, and other non supportive elements of the pet's food out of their body. Certified organic pet food comes with the same environmental benefits as organic human food. The ingredients are grown under strict guidelines, without all of the environmental impacts associated with chemical pesticide and fertilizer production and application.

Human-grade meat products, however, can be tougher on the environment than the by-products from the meat industry that are normally the basis for pet food, since the by-products are leftovers

My Favorite Pet Food

Open Farm is a good brand to consider if you are looking for an organic high-quality protein rich diet. They also have a plant-based variety if you want to feed your pet a meatless diet. Their food is made with ethically sourced, certified humane, and sustainable ingredients; their fish-based food is 100 percent ocean caught, not farmed, and their vegetables are locally sourced. Their packaging is also recyclable through a partnership with Terracycle, a recycling platform offering solutions for eco-minded companies that produce hard-to-recycle materials. Log onto their site to find a retailer near you, to place your order online, and to find out more about their Terracycle recycling program.

that would otherwise just be discarded. So, while "animal bone meal" and "organ meat" sound less than ideal, according to Kelly Scott Swanson, a professor of animal and nutritional sciences in the College of Veterinary Medicine at the University of Illinois, they are nutrient rich and leave a smaller footprint than human-grade ingredients. Also, look for brands that use plant-based ingredients and sustainably certified fish products.

You Made a Conscious Decision to Go Vegetarian or Vegan—Should Your Pets?

If you and your family have committed to a vegetarian or vegan lifestyle based on your culture, religious beliefs, or environmental or health concerns, you may be tempted to include your pets in that practice. Environmentalists point to the fact that cats and dogs are primarily meat-eaters as an example of their negative environmental impact, since livestock used to produce most pet foods are a major source of greenhouse gas emissions.

Many veterinarians advise against feeding your pets a meatless diet, citing their physiological differences and natural feeding habits. There are some, however, who say that a vegetarian diet may be a suitable option for dogs but never for cats. Dr. Ernie Ward of Vet-STREET (www.vetstreet.com) explains that this is because dogs—like humans—are omnivores, which means that they can get their nutrients from a variety of sources, while cats are obligate carnivores and must eat meat to stay healthy.

Since he feels that there is not enough evidence that a completely vegetarian regime is as good for dogs as one that includes meat, Dr. Ward feeds his dogs a "hybrid menu," which includes cooking vegetarian meals for them a few days a week and feeding them meat-based pet food on the other days. If you are already cooking vegetarian meals for your family, this may be a viable option without adding a lot of extra work. You will still need to be mindful of which foods should and should not be included in your dog's meals, but it won't be as complicated as finding adequate protein sources for a completely meatless diet.

Buy Cruelty-Free Pet Food

It seems inconceivable, but many pet food brands test their products on dogs and cats, and the lab animals are often kept under scary conditions. While feeding trials are still standard, many brands have opted not to test on animals. Check to see if your pet's brand is cruelty free.

If the humane treatment of livestock is a concern, but you worry about the possible negative impact of going totally meatless on your pet's health, you may want to explore brands that offer cruelty-free, certified-humane, and sustainable options. Some are even packaged in recyclable materials.

Opt For Green Grooming Supplies and Pet Accessories

The same chemicals that we strive to avoid in our daily lives may be lurking in our pet's grooming products and supplies—the very things we buy to care for them!

Phthalates, the endocrine disruptors found in our personal-care products, are also used in pet shampoos, as well as plastic food bowls, toys, and pill coatings. Not only are they likely to be as harmful to Fluffy and Fido as they are to us, but they can also be transferred to our skin when we wash our pets, even when we have replaced our own personal-care products with phthalate-free alternatives. Phthalates and other harmful additives have also been detected in pet-care runoff water, which ends up in our waterways, resulting in water pollution.

Triclosan, which we talked about earlier in the book and which the FDA banned in 2016 for use in over-the-counter antiseptic hand soaps and body washes, can still be found in shampoos and grooming products made for pets. As with humans, this harmful chemical can easily find its way into their bloodstream through their skin and into our waterways as runoff.

Thankfully, there are now plenty of alternatives to cleansers containing harsh chemicals and toxic additives that are hard on our pets' skin and harmful to us and our water supplies.

To limit your pet's exposure to harmful additives, use natural grooming products—and make sure your grooming salons do as well. Buy food and water bowls made of aluminum or ceramics over plastic, and look for leashes and toys made of recycled and/or recyclable cotton or hemp, which is easy on the soil and doesn't require pesticides to grow.

Bodhi Dog is a family-owned company that produces all-natural, plant-based, eco-responsible, and cruelty-free grooming supplies, using skin-friendly ingredients like essential oils, baking soda, and oatmeal to leave your pets clean, soothed, and smelling fresh. Most of the products can be used on cats as well.

Choose Pesticides and Repellents Carefully

Repelling disease-carrying pests is in the best interests of your family and your pet. However, flea and tick collars can leave harmful residue on our pets' fur for weeks, including chemicals that may cause damage to the nervous system and are even linked to cancer.

These dangers are even worse for children, who are more likely to put their hands in their mouths after touching an animal that has been treated. To reduce the risk of transferring chemical residue, pesticides given in pill form could be a good solution.

Dr. Judy Morgan, a veterinarian and the author of *From Needles to Natural: Learning Holistic Pet Healing*, suggests that essential oils, including lavender, peppermint, lemongrass, and cedar oil, can also be an effective and natural way to deter pests. She advises that essential oils should be diluted in water before being applied to your pet's fur. If you're worried or curious to see if your pet has an allergy to these oils, you can put a few drops in a diffuser and see how your pet reacts. These essential oils can be diluted with virgin olive oil or organic coconut oil. Coconut oil can also be applied directly to your pet to repel fleas and has the added benefit of moisturizing your pet's coat.

Limit your use of essential oils to those that are animal friendly; some, like eucalyptus oil, can be dangerous to dogs and cats. In general, all essential oils should be used with care on cats because of the amount of time they spend grooming, which means the oil can end up in their system. The use of CDB oil has also become popular to keep your pets calm, however, I have not tried it.

Unless your flea problem is extreme, washing your pet and his or her bedding regularly in warm, soapy water—along with vacuuming your home regularly—can go a long way to controlling the problem.

No matter which option you choose, always check your outdoor pets for ticks and be sure to remove them properly. Check with your vet if you are not sure of the most effective way to do that. Lyme disease has become a big problem in certain areas of the United States.

Lawn care treatments for pests can be dangerous to you and your pets since they leave residue on your clothing, your shoes, and your pet's fur, which can then be tracked into your home.

If you still decide that pesticides are needed, look for organic options that use natural bacteria or roundworms to rid your lawn of pests.

Handle Pet Waste Management Responsibly

Waste disposal is a subject often cited by those who believe that keeping pets is detrimental to the environment, and it can't be denied that it poses a dilemma for animal lovers who are also environmentalists. America's dogs produce more than ten million tons of waste each year. Add to that the litter box waste from some ninety million cats and you have a sizeable problem that is on the rise.

According to the EPA, pet waste, and especially waste from dogs, is a "significant" source of water contamination and results in dangerous bacteria, viruses, and pathogens being introduced to our water supplies. The EPA offers some solutions to minimizing the risk of water contamination due to pet waste, which begins with always cleaning up after your pets. A bulletin issued by the EPA says, "The most effective way for pet owners to limit their pet's contribution to source water contamination is to simply clean up and dispose of pet waste." Waste left on sidewalks and streets can end up in storm drains and then be carried out to waterways without being treated.

Also, don't walk your dog near lakes or streams. Instead, go to grassy areas, especially long grass, which helps to filter the waste and provides a safer place for droppings to decompose. Just remember to check for ticks if you do walk them near tall grass.

While composting has been identified as an effective way to manage the growing pet waste problem, animal droppings should not be included in food composting bins, and most experts agree that composting is best left to professional services, where the facilities can maintain the high temperatures necessary to keep the compost safe and pathogen free.

If you decide to engage in DIY pet waste composting in your backyard, it should only be used for landscaping, potted plants, and mulch, but not around plants that are meant to be consumed by humans.

So, what can we do with the dog poo? Flush it, says the EPA. Treatment at most sewage facilities will be able to remove dangerous pathogens from the waste. If that's not practical, or if your community's sewage system isn't designed to handle the removal of dangerous pathogens from pet waste, throwing it in the trash in regular plastic bags is the next best alternative. Although biodegradable waste bags seem like the right way to reduce plastic bags in the landfill, they are designed for composting, not to sit in landfills, where they degrade and emit greenhouse gases.

While flushing is a good alternative for dog waste, you should only flush cat waste if your cat is an indoor cat and has tested negative for toxoplasmosis—a parasitic disease that is dangerous to marine life as well as to pregnant women and those with compromised immune systems.

To reduce the environmental impact of cat litter, avoid those made with clay, which is difficult to extract from soil and doesn't break down effectively. Opt instead for more eco-friendly brands made from corn, wheat, or recycled paper. Or look into a self-cleaning litter box that uses recycled plastic "pebbles" that are automatically washed and reused.

Get Your Community Involved

Some forward-thinking cities have started curbside dog waste composting programs to deal with the growing problem. Lobby your local government officials to see if pet waste composting might be right for your community—either curbside or in public parks.

There are a variety of ways that you can help your pets reduce their environmental paw print so that you can continue to enjoy their companionship and love them as a part of your family while staying true to your green heart plan.

Green Heart Actions

- Rethink how and what you feed your pet. Look for organic foods that are produced humanely and sustainably and consider feeding your dog (but not your cat) vegetarian meals two or three days a week.
- Use the same judgment when buying your pet's grooming products as you do with your own personal care. Avoid shampoos with dangerous additives like phthalates and triclosan, go with natural, organic options for shampoos and sprays, and seek out grooming salons that use them as well.
- Use bedding and toys that are chemical free and are made of recycled and/or recyclable cotton or hemp, which doesn't require pesticides to grow.
- Consider going pesticide free for your lawn by incorporating native plants into your landscaping that will thrive naturally and will keep you, your pets, and the planet healthier.
- Always scoop your pet's poop, flush it when possible, and don't walk dogs near lakes and rivers to avoid water contamination. If you have an indoor cat, look into litter alternatives like those made of corn or recycled paper—or even reusable litter.
- Encourage your community leaders to look into composting programs for pet waste, as some forward-thinking cities have done.

Clothing

We wear our heart's creation.

Growing up, one of my part-time jobs was working in the church thrift shop. I loved foraging through the piles of clothing. At the time I just thought it was great fun and a way to find some great stuff. I had no idea that repurposing these clothes instead of throwing them in the trash was also good for the environment.

The amount of clothing waste we create is incredible. It's estimated that 85 percent of unwanted clothing in the United States goes into a landfill or incinerator and only 15 percent gets donated or recycled. And we're buying more than ever thanks, in part, to fast fashion. Fast fashion is a business model of making fashion trends quickly and cheaply available to consumers. That may sound enticing, but the result is wreaking havoc on the environment. The chemicals used in textile manufacturing produce toxic greenhouse gases as they degrade. The other problem with fast fashion is that the quality is often so poor that thrift shops won't even accept such items as donations.

My current favorite company is Beulah, started by two British women on a trip to India. They have created an apparel company that uses organic materials and employs women in India who have been taken out of sex trafficking, offering them a chance for a new life. Tribute Project is a brand created by Jules Allen and Dani Stone. Their idea was to create one-of-a-kind jackets using deconstructed vintage designer clothing refashioned with custom linings, lyrics, and artwork to create a tribute to a musical artist. Their clothing is designed to tell a story, but the truth is that every piece of clothing you wear tells a story. Part of that story includes the fabric it's made of, the chemicals used in production, where and how it was manufactured, and the waste incurred as a result. If you are not reading the labels and aren't aware of the chemicals that you're putting close to your body and that are eventually being discarded as waste into the environment, the story is not a pretty one.

Read the Label

I've talked a lot throughout this book about the importance of reading labels and knowing what to look for and what to steer clear of. The same holds true when it comes to the clothing you choose.

Many of the toxic chemicals we've discussed that are used in personal-care products and food are also lurking in your clothing. According to Beyond the Label, a shopping guide for healthier fashion, the fashion industry is arguably one of the most polluting industries in the world, using 25 percent of the world's chemicals for textile production and accounting for almost 20 percent of all industrial water pollution. Those chemicals also cause health problems that may start as itchy skin, rashes, eczema, nausea, hives, welts, and migraines, which, depending on the chemicals, may develop into more serious diseases, including cancers and endocrine disruption.

Where to Take Your Clothes When You're Done with Them Instead of the Trash

- Dress for Success
- Housing Works
- Local consignment or thrift store with ethical profit donation practices
- The RealReal
- Tradesy
- ThredUP

When looking for clothing, choose items that are made from recycled, sustainable, chemical-free, organic fabric. A fiber may be labeled "natural," but if it is not produced using ethical and sustainable methods, it may go through a lot of unnatural process to get that way. You can use apps and browser plugins such as Good on You and

Some Clothing Brands and Designers Committed to Ethical Production and Sustainability

- Accompany
- Beulah
- Amour Vert
- Eileen Fisher
- Everlane
- Nisolo
- Patagonia
- Stella McCartney
- Soko
- Reformation

Done Good to help you identify which clothing lines to shop from and which to stay away from. Synthetic fibers like polyester, which first came into commercial use in the early fifties, are a type of plastic made from ethylene, which comes from petroleum. That means that, like plastic bottles, they will not biodegrade.

I don't consider myself a fashionista, but I do believe that what you wear says something about who you are that goes beyond your particular style. Taking the time to make your choices not just on what looks and feels good to wear but also on the way in which it was made, the materials used in the process, and the effect it has on the environment lets the world know you choose to live with a green heart.

Green Heart Actions

- Wear, love, and mend the clothes you have!
- Avoid fast fashion and invest in pieces for long term wear. When looking at price, consider how many times you will wear an item. When you think about cost-per-wear, a better-made, more expensive article of clothing may actually be a better deal.
- Choose organic, eco-friendly fabrics made ethically and using sustainable methods.
- Donate old clothes to a thrift store or give them to a friend instead of throwing them in a recycling bin or the trash.
- Buy second hand and give used clothes another life.
- Support those fashion companies that have good ecological business practices.

The Real Cost of Transportation

Act is an action taking flight.

I fell in love with cars from riding in the back of my parents' Ford Country Squire LTD with its classic wood-paneled exterior. Every summer, my mom loaded my three brothers and me into the wagon to visit my grandparents in Colorado, and she would fold down the backseat so we could stretch out our legs on a foam mattress that she had specially cut for this purpose. Her idea was that we would pass the time quietly reading, but the truth was my three brothers preferred to poke and prod and harass each other, which ultimately gave me the privilege of riding shotgun in the front seat. At the time, no one gave much thought to carbon footprints and climate change and what these gas-guzzling automobiles might do to the environment. All I knew was that there was something about driving on the open road that represented adventures and freedom.

When I moved to California my love affair with driving grew deeper, which was a good thing, since public transportation is not as readily accessible here as it is in some areas. Airplane travel was added to my list of transportation loves when I started working for *Travel + Leisure* magazine, a job that kept me in the air 120 days a year with a territory that included Asia, the Pacific, and the Southwestern United States. All these years later, I still love driving the freeway, and I still get a little thrill out of fastening my seat belt in preparation for a takeoff. The difference now is that I know about greenhouse gas emissions and the damage that excessive use of automobiles and air travel is doing to the atmosphere, so I am constantly on the lookout for ways to curtail and offset my carbon footprint in this area.

Where You Live Matters

When it comes to transportation, it stands to reason that where you live will have a bearing on the size of your carbon footprint. The carbon footprint for a household of four who live in New York City where public transportation is easily accessible and not everyone owns a car can be less than eleven metric tons; for the same-sized household in Los Angeles, the figure rises to more than nineteen.

The good news is that if we're mindful of our transportation options, we can do our part to help the planet.

Drive Sustainably

The auto industry has responded to the increased demand for cleaner, more fuel-efficient cars. Ford is investing $4.5 billion in electrified vehicle solutions, with a plan to add thirteen new electric vehicles to their portfolio by 2020. They've also created a Restricted Substance Management Standard, which prohibits greenhouse gases, and replaced all chlorofluorocarbons refrigerants with hydrofluorocarbons, which do not contribute to ozone depletion and have significantly lower global warming impacts. Part of the reason the 2016 Ford F-150 was awarded Truck of the Year for 2016 by the *Green Car Journal* is its eco-boost engine, which was designed for fuel efficiency and to reduce CO_2 emissions in gasoline-powered vehicles. Having served on the Ford Sustainability Task Force, I know they have taken their commitment to sustainability a step further by introducing initiatives to reduce water usage and recycling enough aluminum scrap to build the equivalent of thirty thousand F-150 truck bodies every month!

But Ford is not alone in its efforts to reduce their carbon footprint and build cars and trucks that perform well, are fuel efficient, and curb greenhouse gas emissions. Toyota introduced the Prius in Japan in 1997, making it the first mass-produced hybrid vehicle. In 2018, the *Green Car Journal* recognized the Cadillac CT6 plug-in as its Connected Green Car of the Year, an award that "acknowledges advanced and environmentally positive vehicles with on-board systems that connect vehicle to driver, to the world, and to the road." Included in the list of runner-ups were the BMW i3, Nissan LEAF, Tesla Model X, and Volvo S90 T8.

Today, there are environmentally friendly choices from every manufacturer, including hybrids that combine gas with battery-powered electric engines, highly efficient internal combustion engines, all-electric models like Tesla, Honda, Mercedes, and Hyundai and hydrogen fuel models.

The rule of thumb, the more fuel-efficient the car, the better for your wallet and for the environment. My dream is to own a Tesla one day and live with a greener heart.

Keep Your Tires Inflated

Desmond Ho, chief scientist at Driving2Save, offers these additional tips to reduce your carbon footprint. Underinflated tires reduce your mileage as much as 10 percent. And every 5 mph over 50 mph is equivalent to $0.21 per gallon in reduced fuel efficiency. Another tip is to repair and maintain your car to keep it performing the most efficiently. Plus, the longer your car lasts, the less resources and carbon emissions are necessary to produce a new one.

Fly Eco-Friendly Skies

A one-way trip from New York's LaGuardia Airport to LAX in Los Angeles drops 1.10 metric tons of CO_2 into the atmosphere. Not good news if you're a frequent flyer, as I am. A great way to neutralize the damage you've done to the atmosphere is to purchase carbon offset credits. This is basically a donation to an organization that will do something to give back to the atmosphere what the CO_2 emissions or greenhouse gases have taken away because of your trip. Carbon offsets are available from a number of sources. My word of caution is that you vet where you're buying your offset from. My favorites are the Better World Club and The Nature Conservancy.

Eco-Hero: Sir Richard Branson

A pioneer in environmental aviation, Sir Richard Branson has done much to keep Virgin Atlantic, the airline he founded, a leader in this area. They have worked with LanzaTech since 2011, using a fermentation process to produce the world's first jet fuel derived from industrial gas waste from steel mills. Early analyses indicate that, compared with conventional jet fuel, the new fuel will result in a carbon savings of 65 percent!

The EPA has a calculator that can help you determine how much damage your trip has done so you can estimate how big an offset credit you want to buy.

Walk, Don't Ride

The greenest ways to get where you're going are walking and bicycling. The next best is taking public transportation when it is available, whether it is the bus, train, light rail, or, if you live in a city like New York, the subway. Carpooling or using shared riding services like Uber and Via are also alternatives to consider. All of these options require a bit more planning and perhaps a bit more time, but that is a small price to pay for helping to lighten your carbon footprint.

Green Heart Actions

- Choose walking, biking, or public transportation whenever possible.
- Use a ride share like Lyft, Uber, Sidecar, Wingz, Summon, Taxify, and Ola Cabs.
- Carpool or investigate peer-to-peer ride sharing.
- When buying your next car, please choose a hybrid, electric, or hydrogen fuel cell vehicle.
- To find the most cost-effective and most eco-friendly car, consult the AAA Green Car Guide from the American Automobile Association or other green car guides.
- New cars often need to off-gas. If you buy a new car, try to find someone to help you do that so you aren't in a toxic car with the windows rolled up and the heater or the air conditioner on.
- Look for a tire that has a high-recycled-material content.

- Buy carbon offsets from the Better World Club, The Nature Conservancy, or another carbon-offset site to balance out the effects of your air travel.
- Try to Skype or video conference as much as you can to lower your carbon footprint.

Socially Responsible Investing and Spending

*I spend and invest my money with companies
that make the world a better place.*

In April 2017, the CVS drugstore chain announced that in response to their customers' requests for safer products and to better align with their mission to help people stay healthy, they would be eliminating parabens, phthalates, and the most prevalent formaldehyde contributors from nearly 600 of their store brand product lines, which include CVS Health, Beauty 360, Essence of Beauty, and Blade. This sort of action is not new for CVS. In 2007, they were the first national retail pharmacy to create a cosmetic safety policy. In 2013, they launched the WERCSmart tool to ensure that product manufacturers register the ingredients in chemically based products. In September 2014, they became the first drugstore chain to stop selling tobacco products, and in 2016, they were the first to sign on with the Chemical Footprint Project, which has a goal of establishing a common metric to assess the progress companies are making toward using safer chemicals as well as transparency in ingredients and production methods.

As we know more about how our environment is affecting our health and how the way we do business is affecting the environment, we demand more transparency and we demand more change. That requires a whole new way of thinking and doing on the part of corporations and the CEOs who are leading them. Profit is important, but it's no longer enough to keep a healthy bottom line and satisfy shareholders, not if the businesses want to retain customers. They have to follow the lead of what companies like CVS are doing.

As people who live with a green heart, you and I can support companies committed to doing the same, whether it is in a personal purchase or in our investment portfolios. We just have to stay aware and continue to read the fine print.

Everyone Can Be a Socially Responsible Investor

You don't have to work on Wall Street or have a large stock portfolio to invest in companies that demonstrate good environmental stewardship. Every purchase you make helps to support those organizations committed to cleaning things up. Everything you do has an impact. That can mean walking one more block to visit an organic dry cleaner instead of one using toxic chemicals, spending a

Mind the Store Retailer Grades

A full list of environmental grades for retailers can be found at the Mind the Store website (retailerreportcard.com), which provides report cards on the actions that retailers are taking to eliminate toxic chemicals in the products they sell.

little extra to buy organic blueberries instead of conventional ones, or asking your financial advisor for sustainable practice information on the companies that make up your 401(k).

Perhaps you do want to buy stocks in a company. It makes sense to put your money where your green heart is. The goal of any investment is to make money, but green investors also want to know the ways in which that business is operating. Responsible investing is not new. According to the Forum for Sustainable and Responsible Investment, by definition socially responsible investing (SRI) is an investment discipline that considers what are known as environmental, social, and governance (ESG) criteria, which are standards that socially conscious investors can do to determine a company's potential to generate long-term competitive financial returns and positive societal impact.

Investing in Those Who Align with Your Values Is Trending

According to the 2016 Report on US Sustainable, Responsible and Impact Investing Trends, as of the end of the year 2015, more than one of every $5 invested, or $8.72 trillion, was invested using SRI strategies. The more demand there is for sustainable and responsible methods of operation and production, the more green change we will see.

As the trend in SRI continues, it is not that hard to find funds that perform well and match your personal green sweet spot. A simple search on the *Barron's* website will get your research started, as will a consultation with your financial advisor, if you have one. For me, I also look at who is heading the fund and their personal commitment to the environment. People like John Streur, CEO of Calvert Investments, considered to be one of the industry leaders in ESG, helps to both define and design ESG principles for a better tomorrow. John is a passionate spokesperson for the rights of indigenous people, gun control policies, issues of inequality, the opioid crisis, among others which are core to the spirit of sustainable investing. His diligent approach of working with shareholders and corporations to resolve greater societal problems, is one of the most effective ways of creating sustainable change because it honors both sides: those who want change and those who can make it happen. Other good ESG firms are Parnassus Investments, Trillium Asset Management and Abacus Wealth Advisors. Your financial advisor can help you find a firm that has ESG investing. Even traditional financial giants like Dimensional Fund Advisors (DFA) and Black Rock have ESG Funds now.

One of the things that is still being worked on in the ESG rating system is incorporating product toxicity into their scores. Because government regulations in transparency in this area continue to lag, third-party organizations are stepping up to the plate. One is the Chemical Footprint Project, whose mission is to create a common metric to assess the progress of companies in reducing the use of chemicals of high concern and increasing the use of safer alternatives. The first survey was launched in 2015 with participation voluntary. The results are based on management strategy, chemical inventory, footprint measurement, and disclosure and verification.

Another is Mind the Store, a coalition of NGOs that ranks companies on chemical policy, transparency, and continued improvement in actions to eliminate toxins and gives them a report-card-style grade. At the head of the class in 2017 was Apple with an *A*.

In the end, it's up to us to be conscious consumers and responsible investors if we want to have an impact on the environment. That might require taking an eco-pause before you add that container of milk to your shopping cart, walking an extra block to support a retailer you know is making efforts to reduce its chemical footprint, or spending some extra time reading beyond the financial performance on a fund you want to invest it. I assure you that taking more time now will increase your chances of having more time later in good health.

Green Heart Actions

- When shopping, spend your money with companies that are committed to environmental stewardship, sustainable business practices, and social governance supporting gender diversity and indigenous people.
- When investing in publicly traded companies, choose an investment firm that has SRI portfolios based on solid ESG scores and supports shareholder advocacy.

GET INVOLVED

I choose to live consciously and share lovingly.

According to an article in the *New York Times*, as of January 31, 2018, there were sixty-seven environmental rules that had either already been overturned or were in danger of being rolled back during the months in which I wrote this book, in the Trump administration. This included the antidumping rule for coal companies, the offshore drilling ban in the Atlantic and Arctic Oceans, Green Climate Fund contributions, and the reusable water bottle rule for national parks. Just recently, the FDA withdrew the Organic Livestock and Poultry Practices Rule, which had been delayed from implementation after it was finalized in January 2017. These regulations would have improved the quality of animal care for products earning the "organic" label, including specifying minimums for indoor and outdoor space for chickens and prohibiting inhumane practices such as de-beaking. None of this makes my green heart happy, but it does make me more committed than ever to stay involved in making the world a greener, healthier, and safer place through increasing my work with private and public companies as well as other institutions, schools and most importantly, you. It is my hope that by learning more about your environment and the threat we are all under in today's world, you might be motivated to do the same. There are many ways to do that beyond what we've discussed in this book, including donating time, financially supporting environmental organizations, and becoming politically active.

Vote with a Green Heart

During his gap year before college, my son Colin went to work as an intern for Gavin Newsom, who was running for governor of California at the time. Colin is majoring in International Relations at the University of Pennsylvania, and is interested in domestic and international policy and environmental justice. I am proud of Colin for his passion to help change the world. He worked long hours and learned a lot from his boss and Newsom Finance Director, Katie Prisco-Buxbaum. He told me that one of the most important things he learned, beyond the fact that political campaigns in the U.S. burn through a lot of cash, was how Gavin listened to his constituents and relied on them to learn about key public issues. Seeing Gavin in action on the campaign trail, demonstrated to him how very important it is for all of us who are of voting age to get involved in our local and national issues to help be a part of the change.

What many people fail to realize is that grassroots, local, and state representation is where change starts. It took me a long time to feel comfortable with being political because I don't like conflict, but what I have come to realize in life is that becoming educated about issues is the only way to come to a true decision about what's best for you. If you give up that right you are letting someone else make the decision for you, someone who may or may not have your best interests at heart.

I encourage you to find out who is running for office and where they stand on environmental issues. I am getting more involved in The League of Conservation Voters (origin.lcv.org), through one of my dearest and most trusted eco-girlfriends, Laura Seydel. Carol Browner,

Gene Karpinski, and the LCV team, are passionate about supporting the environment and working through the legislative processes to make the world a safer, healthier place. In September of 2018, Stacey Folsom, Senior Vice President for Development, told me they had over two million members and 35,000 volunteers who had taken over 2.8 million actions to improve the world. They also have a great Scorecard, called Give Green, if you want to find out how your favorite political candidate views environmental and other important social issues.

Stay Informed

One of the purposes of this book is to educate. But it's not enough. With so many of the laws and regulations having been written by lawyers and lobby groups in language that is hard to decipher, with deregulation groups trying to roll back legislation designed to protect you, and with new research being uncovered every day, the onus is on you to find the truth. Environmental nonprofits are a wonderful source. They're on the green front lines and know where the hot spots are, where you can be of the most help, and what you should watch out for.

Here are some of my favorite organizations:

- **CAPTAIN PLANET FOUNDATION**—This is my favorite children's environmental cause. Started by my friend Laura Turner Seydel, Captain Planet raises money to create school gardens nationwide that help students learn how to grow, cook, eat, and understand what foods are healthy. With a tiny staff and a mighty ambition, in 2018 they funded nearly 3,000 school gardens.
- **ENVIRONMENTAL WORKING GROUP (EWG)**—A nonprofit, non-partisan organization led by Ken Cook, EWG shares my green mission to help you lead a healthier life in a healthier

environment by empowering you with accurate information. Their team of scientists, lawyers, and policy experts has not only delivered groundbreaking research and fought in Washington for legislation that protects consumers from toxins and chemicals in products, but they also have created the mark, which is designed to help make it easier for you to make healthy, green choices.

- **NATURAL RESOURCES DEFENSE COUNCIL**—Cofounded by John Adams, the council has been around since 1970, with a mission to protect your rights to clean air, clean water,

More Environmental Groups Worth Supporting

- Bioneers
- Center for Environmental Health
- Conservation International
- Earth Justice
- Friend of the Sea
- Global Green
- Kiss the Ground
- Marine Stewardship Council
- Monterey Bay Aquarium
- Plastic Pollution Coalition
- Rachel's Network
- Sustainable Food Trust
- TerraCycle
- The Ellen MacArthur Foundation
- The Nature Conservancy
- The Ocean Trust
- The Rodale Institute
- The Socially Responsible Agriculture Project

and environmentally healthy communities. Not only can you help support their work through donations, but their website directs you to a list of environmental issues that are on the table and who you can call or write to in the government to make your voice heard.

- **NEW FUTURE SUMMIT**—Founded by Zem Joaquin of Ecofabulous. Her conference brings together inventors, entrepreneurs, media, and investors and the tools to change the world.
- **THE RACHEL CARSON NETWORK**—Inspired by the pioneer activist, Rachel Carson, author of *Silent Spring*. It is a community of women funders lead by Fern Shepard, committed to a safer, healthier, and more just world for all.
- **THE LEAGUE OF CONSERVATION VOTERS (LCV)**—LCV understands that threats to our environment and our democracy are interlinked. We will not solve the many environmental challenges we face without first winning the politics: securing strong policies, holding leaders accountable, and winning key elections. With more than thirty state partners and millions of supporters across the country, LCV works to build a world where government at all levels works to protect the water we drink, the air we breathe, the lands we love, and the future of the planet we call home.
- **THE LEONARDO DICAPRIO FOUNATION**—The LDF Foundation, through its collaborative partnerships, supports innovative projects that protect vulnerable wildlife from extinction, while restoring balance to threatened ecosystems and communities. Their work is divided into six main program areas: Wildlands Conservation, Oceans Conservation, Climate Change, Indigenous Rights, Transforming California, and Innovative Solutions.
- **THE UNITED NATIONS FOUNDATION**—This foundation is headed by Kathy Calvin and was originally funded by Ted

Turner with a billion dollar gift for the purpose of broadening support for the UN through advocacy and public outreach. It is now supported by philanthropic, corporate, government and individual donors to connect people, ideas and resources to help the UN solve global challenges from climate change to universal health access to women's empowerment.

- **WATERKEEPER ALLIANCE**—The largest and fastest growing nonprofit solely focused on clean water. They work with more than two hundred local Waterkeepers located at fresh waters and bays around the United States, and they are growing internationally. A few years ago, they put out an app to tell you the water safety level in your area. Clean water is the basis of all living things on this planet.

Share What You Know on Social Media

Social media can be a positive force for change. Share what you know. Follow the environmental groups that are most important to you. Help to spread the word that climate change is real and that clean air, water, and food, and products produced without harmful chemicals and toxins are a right, not a privilege.

Green Heart Actions

- Join a community or national nonprofit that is cleaning up or preserving the environment; they all need your help.
- Start a group within your neighborhood to share environmental concerns, resources, or education.
- Help someone who isn't sure how to start living an eco-friendly life.

SO, WHAT DO I DO NOW?

I live with a green heart.

I hope this book will give you permission to create a healthier personal environment for you and for those around you. If each of us does this for our own environment, the greater environment will get cleaned up and we as a planet can heal, making all life healthier. Good environmental stewardship starts with good environmental leadership, which starts with you.

Cleaning up your environment might mean that you may have to enlist a spouse or partner or roommate to help you. You might have to get coworkers together to meet with the building management to ask them to test the water and air and furniture in your working space to ensure that it's healthy. You might have to knock on the doors of your neighbors or ask members of your church or school or community to help you look into the environmental health of your shared space. You might feel compelled to call your councilperson, your mayor, your governor, your congressman, or your senator to make sure your community is environmentally safe. It is both your right and your responsibility to make sure that your family and you are not exposed to toxins without your knowledge. As Margaret Mead said,

"Never doubt that a small group of thoughtful, committed citizens can change the word; indeed, it's the only thing that ever has."

This book to save the world really isn't about saving the whole world. It is a book about saving your own world, the environment in which you live, your body and personal environment around you. It will take the collective force of public, private, and individual efforts all working together to clean up our world. I hope you will join me in making this possible, by taking one green heart action at a time.

Live, love, and vote with a Green Heart!

GLOSSARY

ALKALINE: Alkaline solutions are basic and therefore possess the opposite properties of acids. Many ionic minerals found in natural water sources, such as magnesium ($Mg2+$) and calcium ($Ca++$) are alkalizing and raise the pH of water above seven. There is evidence to support that drinking ionized, alkaline water is beneficial to human health.

ALLOPATHIC MEDICINE: A western school of medicine that uses a systems-based approach to cure illness by addressing the patient's symptoms.

ALTERNATIVE ENERGY: Energy from sources that do not deplete natural resources, such as solar, wind, biomass, or geothermal energy sources.

ALTERNATIVE FUELS: Vehicle fuels that are non-petroleum based, including biodiesel, ethanol, electricity, and hydrogen.

ANTIBIOTIC FREE: Farmers have historically used antibiotics to prevent or treat existing disease in their livestock. However, the widespread, unnecessary use of preventative antibiotic treatment in livestock is increasingly threatening to public health. Products that are labeled "antibiotic free" or "raised without antibiotics" (several variations of this label exist) suggest to the consumer that the meat or poultry in question was never treated with antibiotics during its lifetime. While numerous labels may claim a product is "antibiotic free", only one of these variations "no antibiotics added" is enforced or sanctioned by the USDA.

ANTIOXIDANTS: Natural or synthetic compounds that reduce human cell damage through neutralizing oxygen free radicals (a natural byproduct of cellular respiration). Fruits and vegetables are natural sources of antioxidants.

ARTIFICIALLY COLORED: Synthetic colors or dyes are often added to food products in order to make them more appealing, distinguishable, or to achieve a color similar to what the food looked like before processing. Artificial dyes can be found in many grocery store products, especially baked or processed goods, as well as fish and meat products. Color additives must be certified as safe to ingest by the FDA before being used commercially. Still the safety of several of these chemical additives is questionable and numerous color additives have been banned in the past for their carcinogenic effects such as Quinoline Yellow (Yellow #10) and Red #4.

ASPARTAME: An artificial sweetener (also known as Equal* and NutraSweet*) that is believed to be toxic in high amounts.

BIOACCUMULATION: The process by which toxins such as Mercury, pesticides, PBC's, and dioxins build up in fish and other seafood products. When a larger fish eats smaller contaminated fish, it retains the toxins present in the smaller fish and the process continues on until the fish at the top of the food chain has accumulated a high density of toxins. As humans, we are at the top of the food chain, and therefore we ingest all of the chemicals that have built up in our seafood products.

BIOCIDE: Either a natural or synthetic chemical or microorganism used to control or render other biological means; a pesticide, antimicrobial, disinfectant, preservative, or others.

BIODEGRADABLE: Materials that are capable of being broken down by natural processes, such as decomposition by microorganisms and fungi, and reabsorbed back into the environment are biodegradable.

BIODIESEL: An alternative fuel derived from biological sources. Biodiesel is usually produced from virgin or recycled vegetable oils. Biodiesel is cleaner option than petrol-diesel because it releases less carbon monoxide, aromatic hydrocarbons, and particulate matter (soot) upon combustion.

BIODYNAMIC: A farming method whose modern practice began about seventy years ago that uses basic organic farming practices with the addition of special plant, animal, and mineral soil preparations. Biodynamic farmers strive to follow the rhythms of the Earth and its seasons in order to create a self-supporting, harmonic ecosystem.

BPA: BPA, short for Bisphenol A, is a chemical utilized in the production of plastics that have been found to have a toxic effect on the brain and nervous system. Research into the safety of exposure to BPA in small amounts is ongoing.

CAGE-FREE: The term "cage-free" is typically used in reference to the housing conditions of egg-laying hens that are utilized in mass production. Cage-free systems arose as a more humane alternative to the battery cage systems that have served as the industry standard for housing hens for years. When the public became aware of the cruel and torturous nature of battery cage systems, farmers began to adopt more humane cage-free containment models. While cage-free systems are not regulated by any governing agency and do not necessarily allow hens access to the outdoors, nor ensure the animals are treated without cruelty, the hens contained in cage-free systems are at least afforded enough space to stretch their wings, walk, perch, and otherwise act naturally.

CARBON BLACK: A powder that may be found in eyeliner and other makeup products that is considered toxic and possibly carcinogenic. This compound also goes by the name of acetylene black, channel black, D & C black no. 2, and furnace black.

CARBON FOOTPRINT: Calculating the "carbon footprint" of an individual, family, or company is one way to quantify the amount of carbon waste that they produce in the form of greenhouse gases, primarily Carbon Dioxide (CO_2) gas, both directly and indirectly on an annual basis. A "carbon footprint" is typically measured in tons of CO_2 per unit of time and is a useful measure in considering our personal impact, or the impact of a larger entity, on the environment. Key contributors include transportation, electricity use, and diet.

CARBON MONOXIDE GAS: A tasteless, odorless gas that is highly toxic to human life and a natural byproduct of petrol combustion. Carbon monoxide gas is also used as an additive to commercially sold fish, because the gas slows the natural discoloration of the product, making the fish appear fresh for longer.

CARBON OFFSET: While modern daily life necessitates the production of a certain amount of carbon waste, one way to remediate the amount of carbon dioxide produced (also known as one's carbon footprint) is to invest time and/or resources in projects dedicated to improving global environmental health. These environmentally-positive projects include such endeavors as rainforest restoration or protection, planting trees, or promoting the development of new renewable energy plants or resources. Investment in these projects with the aim of "making up for" carbon emissions is referred to as a "carbon offset" and is one way of moving toward carbon neutrality.

CARCINOGEN: A substance or chemical that promotes the development or growth of cancerous cells.

CASEIN: A protein found in milk.

CHLOROFLUOROCARBONS (CFCS): A class of chemicals frequently used in the production of aerosols among other commercial products. While these compounds are relatively safe as they are meant to be used, upon reaching the upper atmosphere, CFCs rapidly destroy ozone through a natural chemical reaction.

CIRCULAR ECONOMY: A new way of approaching economic growth that seeks to reduce the consumption and subsequent waste of precious resources by focusing instead on renewable energy, recycling or repurposing products that are already in circulation, and returning the planet to a more sustainable state.

COLD-PRESSED: The process of "cold-pressing" juice, nut butters, or oils is unique among processing or juicing methods in that it minimally alters the nutrient composition of the final product. Because a cold-press juicer or strainer gently grinds or "chews" produce, it is able to separate the plant fiber (which is tough and chewy) from the rest of the plant cell contents. This means that essential nutrients, enzymes, sugars, and vitamins originally present in the produce are far less likely to be damaged than if subjected to other common juicing methods (that require sharp blades or heat) and will remain in the final product. As the name suggests, "cold-press" methods do not use heat to extract additional juice or oil. Therefore the final product remains truly raw and its proteins are not subjected to heat, ensuring that enzymes are still "live" or functional.

CONVENTIONALLY GROWN: Produce that is grown with the use of pesticides, or other chemicals.

DEMETER CERTIFIED: Demeter International is a nonprofit organization that seeks to heal the environment by supporting biodynamic farmers and their products.

DIOXINS (POLYCHLORINATED DIBENZODIOXINS): A group of toxic chemicals that are byproducts of burning waste, as well as forest fires (as well as other processes), and are persistent in the environment (do not decompose). According to the U.S. Environmental Protection Agency (EPA), dioxins have a toxic effect on human systems and are known carcinogens.

DIRECT TRADE: Though not a formal certification, direct trade is a term often used when coffee roasters buy beans directly from farmers. Boutique roasters and coffee shops create these direct relationships in order to improve farmer profits and to gain better control of crop quality and farming methods.

EMFS: Electromagnetic fields, or EMFs, are invisible energy fields that arise as a natural consequence of using electricity. EMF radiation can be either non-ionizing (non-harmful to humans) or ionizing (harmful to humans).

ENDOCRINE DISRUPTOR: Any chemical that interferes with the endocrine system, which produces and regulates all hormones in the body. Endocrine disruptors come in many forms and can be found in food, plastic, and other products that we come into contact with every day. They have the potential to cause damage to human health as well as the health of wildlife and the environment.

ENVIRONMENTAL WORKING GROUP (EWG): A nonprofit organization that seeks to create a healthier world and environment through education, awareness, and research initiatives.

ENRICHED: When foods are "enriched" it means that certain essential nutrients, such as vitamins and minerals, are added back into the product after its natural nutrients have been stripped away by processing. Despite enrichment, these processed foods often lack whole nutrition necessary for health. This method is often applied to wheat or other products made of grain, such as bread, cereal, or other flour products.

EXTRA-VIRGIN: Oils that are cold-pressed, free of chemical additives, and haven't been heated above 27 degrees Celsius during processing, are considered extra-virgin. Olive oils are held to additional standards in the US that require the free fatty acid content of the product to be at or below 0.5 percent.

FAIR TRADE: The fair trade initiative seeks to help farmers in the developing world get a fair price for their crops and helps to maintain humane working conditions, agricultural traditions, and ecological diversity.

FARM-RAISED (AQUACULTURE): In the context of modern food production, "farm-raised" most commonly refers to artificial cultivation of seafood for human consumption. In general, fish-farming operations cultivate a captive population of whichever species they intend to farm, among the most common are salmon and tilapia, by breeding, artificially feeding, and eventually harvesting the farmed species within a wired or netted area of coastal ocean or other large body of water. This method of farm-raising seafood products, also referred to as "aquaculture," has grown in popularity in recent years due to the decline of natural and wild resources available to an ever growing consumer market.

FDA: The United States Food and Drug Administration (FDA) is a governmental agency under the umbrella of the U.S. Department of Health and Human Services that seeks to ensure a safe and reliable food supply for the United States, as well as to oversee the development and approval of new and existing pharmaceuticals and medical devices.

FORMALDEHYDE: A well-known human carcinogen that is found in many commercial products from nail polish to plywood.

FORTIFIED: Foods that are fortified have certain vitamins and minerals added to them that were not initially in the food before processing.

Common examples of food fortification are the addition of Vitamin D to milk and folate to flour products.

FREE-RANGE: The term free-range (as it used in food labeling) applies specifically to poultry raised in the United States, and is under the regulation of the USDA. In order to be free-range compliant, poultry farmers must allow their birds "access" to the outdoors. However neither the amount nor quality of "outdoor time" allowed to the birds is specified by the USDA. Because this definition is quite vague in its wording, free-range poultry can generally be considered more humane, although it is difficult to determine to what degree due to the lack of detailed regulation.

FUNGICIDE: A chemical compound which is also called an antimycotic; a substance used to kill the growth of fungi. See biocide.

FURAN (POLYCHLORINATED DIBENZOFURAN): A member of the dioxin family of toxins that is carcinogenic.

GLUTEN: A class of proteins found in many grains, and a variety of other foods, that help the plant maintain its shape. Common sources of gluten include, but are not limited to, bread, pasta, cereal, baked goods and food products made of wheat flour, barley, and rye.

GMO (GENETICALLY MODIFIED ORGANISM): Any organism that has had its genetic makeup artificially altered may be considered a "GMO" or genetically modified organism. However, this term is most commonly used in reference to produce or other food products that originate from genetically altered crops or seeds. One way that farmers and scientists have collaborated to promote crop yield over the past several decades is through the development of genetically modified seeds capable of resisting traditional plights, such as insect infestation. By inserting desirable genes into the seeds of the crops that are to be cultivated through recombinant DNA technology (or "gene-splicing"), such as resistance to a certain pesticide, these crops are able to survive the administration of pesticides that would otherwise kill the plant. In this way, farmers are able to eliminate pests that would potentially reduce their crop yield without damaging the produce itself. Among the most common GMO crops grown in the U.S. are soy, canola, and corn.

GRAINS: Members of the grains group include (but are not limited to) wheat, barley, rice, oats, and cornmeal. Grain products, such as bread, can be made with either whole grain (unprocessed, original nutrients intact) or refined grains, which have had their natural fiber, iron, and vitamins removed.

GRASSFED: According to the American Grassfed Association (AGA), the criteria for livestock to be considered grassfed are that the animals have eaten only grass after an initial weaning stage, have never been given artificial hormones or antibiotics, and have been raised with enough room to naturally graze and roam.

GRAY WATER: Any water that has been used in the home, except water from toilets, is called graywater. Dish, shower, sink, and laundry water comprise 50 to 80 percent of residential "waste" water that may be used for other purposes, such as landscape irrigation, and can significantly reduce the use of fresh water.

GREENHOUSE GASES: A collective term for gases whose chemical properties allow them to trap heat in the atmosphere as they absorb infrared light creating the "greenhouse effect." Methane, carbon dioxide, and fluorocarbons are all common examples of greenhouse gases.

HEAVY METALS: Dense, metallic elements that are naturally found in the Earth's crust but are toxic or poisonous to humans in relatively low concentrations. Several common heavy metals that humans may be exposed to through water, food products, and the environment are mercury (Hg), cadmium (Cd), arsenic (Ar), chromium (Cr), and lead (Pb).

HERBICIDE: A chemical agent used to kill or inhibit the growth of vegetation. (See biocide.)

HOMEOPATHIC: A holistic approach to medicine that aims to treat the whole person, as opposed to only treating the area exhibiting symptoms, with natural remedies.

HORMONE FREE: Another farming practice that has come under scrutiny in recent years is the administration of hormones to livestock in order to increase their rate of growth and, in the case of dairy cows, their milk production. While the USDA prohibits the use of hormones in raising poultry and pork, cattle and dairy farmers in the United States are still allowed to administer synthetic hormones, the most common being rBST (recombinant bovine somatotropin), also referred to as rBGH (recombinant Bovine Growth Hormone), to their livestock. There is growing concern that the presence of rBST in milk and beef can be detrimental to both human health as well as the health of the livestock. Several federal certifications such as organic, humane, and grass-fed ensure that certified producers do not use hormones during the animal's lifespan. It is important to note that "hormone free" milk and meat products do not technically exist, as there are many natural hormones produced by the livestock still present in the final product sold in grocery stores, such as estrogen. However, according to the USDA, products may be labeled as "no hormones added" if no hormones are administered to the livestock during their lifetime.

HUMANE FARM ANIMAL CARE (HFAC): A nonprofit organization created to promote the humane treatment of livestock that provides a Certified Humane certification to farmers who verifiably meet their high standards for animal care. They also independently certify labels such as "free range" and "pasture raised."

LACTOSE: A sugar naturally found in milk.

LED (LIGHT EMITTING DIODE) LIGHTING: An alternative to incandescent and fluorescent lighting that is more energy efficient, produces less waste, and is gentler on the environment.

LOCALLY GROWN: While "locally grown" may be a subjective definition, locally grown products are generally associated with a greater level of freshness, a decrease in greenhouse gases due to fewer transportation miles and less refrigeration, and supportive of local economies and small businesses. However, neither the USDA nor FDA define or regulate the use of the terms "local" or "locally grown" in food labeling. It is also important to note that, while "locally grown" foods are generally considered healthier and more responsible purchases, this label does not speak to the use of pesticides, GMOs, hormones, or any other methods of food manipulation during the production process. Therefore, it is important to consider the methods of food production separately from where they are produced.

MELANOMA: A cancer of melanocytes, or human pigment cells, usually found in the skin.

METHANE: An organic gas that is composed of one carbon atom and four hydrogen atoms produced by bacteria present in the digestive tract of many animals (such as humans and cows).

NATURAL: The term "natural" is not formally defined by the FDA in its use in human food labeling, therefore it can essentially be used and interpreted at the discretion of the manufacturer. While the FDA does not formally regulate the use of "natural" in labeling, this agency has indicated that they consider the term "natural" to mean that nothing artificial has been introduced to the food product.

NOAA: The National Oceanic and Atmospheric Administration (NOAA) is a sector of the US Department of Commerce that manages weather forecasts and emergency storm warnings nationwide, in addition to the economic and ecological health of our nation's fisheries and coastline.

NON-GMO PROJECT VERIFIED: The Non-GMO Project is a nonprofit foundation created to combat the spread of GMOs in agriculture and protect the non-GMO crops that remain. Products bearing the label "non-GMO project verified" have been vetted by a third-party administrator that has verified that they do not contain any GMOs.

NONTOXIC: We can generally assume that the "nontoxic" products that we put on our skin or use in our home are free of chemicals and substances that are known to be harmful to human health.

OCHRONOSIS: A disorder of the skin that manifests as blue and black discoloration and may be caused by the topical application of creams or other substances that contain hydroquinone.

ORGANIC: For products to be labeled "organic" they must meet certain federally regulated criteria. Organic regulations are among the most strict in our national food system and are constantly under scrutiny from the National Organic Standards Board (NOSB) which seeks to ensure that all organic produce is grown without pesticides, artificial fertilizers, genetically modified seeds, or detriment to the soil and water sources.

Additionally, organic livestock, poultry, dairy, and eggs must be free of added hormones and antibiotics. Farmers are inspected by the USDA to ensure that they meet all criteria.

OSTEOPATHIC: Osteopathy, or osteopathic medicine, is a western model of medicine that is in most ways identical to the allopathic model except for the additional training Osteopaths receive in hands-on diagnosis and treatment called osteopathic manipulative medicine (OMM) and a focus on overall wellness.

PARABENS: A family of organic preservatives commonly used in cosmetics and food.

PASTURE RAISED: Pasture raised animals are allowed access to the outdoors, however there are no current federal standards for the quantity of time spent outdoors nor the quality of the pasture available to the animals. Term is not synonymous with "grassfed" as these animals may be fed grain or other animal feed.

PASTEURIZATION: A method of partially-sterilizing liquids, most commonly dairy products, with heat high enough to kill pathogenic microorganisms, but retain the original quality and taste of the product.

PATHOGEN: Broadly speaking, a pathogen is any agent that causes disease. Microorganisms such as fungi and bacteria that cause infection and/or disease are considered "pathogenic."

PERFLUOROOCTANOIC ACID (PFOA): A toxic, environmentally persistent chemical utilized in the production of teflon.

PESTICIDES: Chemicals that are designed to protect commercial crops by repelling and/or killing insects, microorganisms, or any other pests that might eat or damage the crops.

PH: The pH scale was created to measure the acidity or basicity of a substance. The scale ranges from 1 to 14, with 1 being the most acidic value and 14 being the most basic. Pure, distilled water has a pH of 7 and is the neutral midpoint of the pH scale.

PHOTOVOLTAIC: A solar power technology that uses solar cells to convert light from the sun into electricity.

PHTHALATES: A group of chemicals frequently used in the production of flexible plastics, as well as personal products such as shampoo, cosmetics, and nail polish.

PHYTOCHEMICALS: A broad term for chemicals that are naturally found in plants. Phytochemicals may be helpful or detrimental to human health, depending on the nature of the chemical in question. Several examples of innocuous phytochemicals that we commonly ingest include carotenoids, flavonoids, and terpenes.

PHYTOESTROGENS: A group of phytochemicals that weakly mimic the effects of human estrogen. Phytoestrogens are most commonly found in soy products, and can act as endocrine disruptors.

POLYTETRAFLUOROETHYLENE (PTFE): A compound, also known as Teflon, that is highly inert, which is why it is often used as a nonstick surface for cookware.

POLYVINYL CHLORIDE (PVC): PVC is commonly used to produce plastic pipes and outdoor furniture. It is seldom, if ever, recyclable and its synthesis creates toxic byproducts, such as dioxins. Additionally, PVC plastics often contain phthalates, another toxic group of chemicals that make plastics soft and flexible.

POLYETHYLENE GLYCOL: A solvent commonly used in personal care products including cosmetics, sunscreen, moisturizers, and antiperspirant that may have a toxic effect on human organ systems.

PRESERVATIVES: A group of chemicals that slow or delay the natural decomposition of commercial products and foodstuffs. Common preservatives include sodium benzoate, sodium sulfite, propyl paraben, and butylated hydroxytoluene (BHT).

PROBIOTICS: Healthy gut bacteria that positively interact with the human host by promoting digestion and improving immune strength.

PROCESSED: As a rule of thumb, the more processed a food product is, the farther away it is from its natural, whole state. In general, foods may be referred to as "processed" if they have undergone physical and/or chemical alteration.

PROPYLENE GLYCOL: A synthetic compound that absorbs water and is commonly used as an antifreeze agent.

PROJECT DRAWDOWN: A movement created to reverse climate change by implementing existing methods of reducing carbon waste and actively investigating new, practical ways to heal our environment.

RAINFOREST ALLIANCE: A private, non-profit organization that promotes sustainable agriculture, responsible forestry, and eco-tourism through its certification and labeling system.

RAW: Produce that remains uncooked or unheated. In the context of the raw food movement, a food is "raw" if it has not been cooked or heated above 118 degrees Fahrenheit.

RECOMBINANT BOVINE SOMATOTROPIN (rBST): A synthetic hormone based on bovine somatotropin that is administered to commercial dairy cows in order to promote milk production, as well as to cattle intended to be sold as meat in order to increase their rate of growth. This hormone is also referred to as recombinant bovine growth hormone (rBGH).

RENEWABLE ENERGY CERTIFICATE: Also known as renewable energy credits, these tradable commodities certify that one megawatt hour of electricity has been generated renewably and fed into the power grid.

RESPONSIBLY SOURCED: Foods that are generally produced and sold by sellers, growers, and companies that believe their practices are socially and environmentally conscious. Foods that are considered to be "responsibly sourced" have numerous economic and environmental benefits, however these benefits are not guaranteed by any regulating entity.

SATURATED FATS: Fats that are solid at room temperature, such as butter and animal fat, are generally saturated fats. Because the hydrocarbon chains of these fatty acids have no double bonds (i.e. are completely "saturated" by hydrogen atoms), they stack tightly against one another causing them to be more rigid and maintain their shape. Ingesting high amounts of saturated fats over time is generally associated with an increased risk of developing cardiovascular disease, among other chronic health challenges.

SILOXANES: Silicon-based compounds that can be found in toothpaste, moisturizers, hair products, deodorants, cosmetics, and lubricants. Siloxanes are known endocrine disruptors and may also be reproductive toxins.

SOCIALLY RESPONSIBLE INVESTING/INVESTMENTS (SRI): An approach to investing that seeks to maximize financial returns alongside social and environmental benefits.

SOLAR PANELS: Panels constructed of photovoltaic cells that capture and utilize the sun's energy to heat homes, pools, or otherwise provide energy.

SPROUTING: The process of soaking seeds, legumes, nuts, or grains in water for several hours and then repeatedly rinsing them until they begin to sprout, or grow. By sprouting seeds before they are eaten, the amount of available nutrients is increased and their mildly toxic components, such as lectins or saponins, decrease in concentration.

SULFATE: A chemical group used commercially in strong detergents that strip away oil or grease, most commonly in the form Sodium Lauryl Sulfate (SLS). SLS can be found in many personal products that produce a "foam," such as shampoos and facial cleansers.

SUPERFOOD: Food products that are believed to have an exceptionally positive impact on human health.

SUSTAINABLE: In general, a sustainable practice is one that can be maintained over time at a constant level or pace.

TOLUENE: An organic solvent used in paint, nail polish, adhesives, plastics, and rubber (to name a few) that is toxic to the human nervous system. Prolonged exposure to toluene can cause symptoms such as confusion, dizziness, and impaired coordination.

TRANS-FATS: Trace amounts of trans-fats are naturally present in red meat and dairy, but the trans-fats present in most grocery store products are artificially synthesized from vegetable oils through a process called "hydrogenation." That is why trans-fats are also referred to as "hydrogenated fats/oils." These fats are associated with an increased risk of heart disease and the development of diabetes.

TRIPHENYL PHOSPHATE (TPP/TPHP): A chemical found in "nontoxic" nail polish that aims to replace the original three toxins used in nail polish (toluene, formaldehyde, and dibutyl phthalate). However, new data suggests that TPP is similarly toxic and acts as a potent endocrine disruptor. Preliminary studies performed in animal models have shown that TPP exposure can lead to obesity, anxiety, and other health problems.

ULTRA-HIGH TEMPERATURE (UHT): An alternative method of pasteurizing dairy products that utilizes higher temperatures (greater than 280 degrees Fahrenheit) for a longer period of time (>2 seconds) than traditional pasteurization techniques, which is thought to kill a greater amount of bacteria.

UNSATURATED FATS: Fats that are liquid at room temperature, such as olive oil and other plant-derived oils, are generally unsaturated fats. Because the hydrocarbon chains of these fatty acids have double bonds (i.e., are not completely "saturated" by hydrogen atoms), they are less tightly packed against one another, which allows these fats to be more fluid. Unsaturated fats are generally regarded as a healthier choice than saturated fats or trans-fats.

USDA: The United States Department of Agriculture (USDA) is a governmental body that came into being in 1862 and continues today to utilize new scientific data in order to inform public policy in regard to agriculture, food, and nutrition.

VEGAN: A lifestyle and/or diet that involves avoiding foods, clothing, and other daily items that are derived from animal products.

VOLATILE ORGANIC COMPOUNDS (VOCS): VOCs are emitted as gases from certain solids or liquids. VOCs are especially hazardous indoors, where concentrations may be up to ten times higher than outdoors. New carpet, paint, and interior finishes are common sources of VOCs in the home. Look for products labeled "low-VOC," "no-VOC," or "zero-VOC."

WATERKEEPER ALLIANCE: A nonprofit organization that strives to hold water polluters accountable for their actions and unite clean water rights activists around the world to achieve their goal of "drinkable, fishable, swimmable water everywhere."

WILD CAUGHT: Fish that are wild caught are caught by commercial fishermen in their natural habitat. They may or may not be responsibly sourced, but they are often a healthier option than farmed fish because their diet and lifestyle are natural throughout their lifetime.

ACKNOWLEDGMENTS

I was a toddler when Rachel Carson's book *Silent Spring* was published (1962). Her story was the beginning of the environmental health movement, and she has been followed by many other courageous people who fight every day to keep our world healthy. I am grateful for her work and the work of others, including eco-heroes like Erin Brockovich, and have written this book in support of them, picking up the baton where Rachel left off and carrying it forward.

I wrote this book out of love and pain for what I have experienced and seen while living on this planet in my five decades. I could not have written it without the encouragement of Jennifer Freed, who gave me the confidence to pick up my pen again thirty years after my college writing days. The book was written on planes and trains and automobiles as well as some buses, boats, and bikes; while staying in a refurbished chicken coop, numerous hotels, and guest rooms of many friends and relatives. It never left my thoughts or my side for nine months. In some ways, it is my fourth child.

I owe heartfelt thanks to Sadhguru, who taught me Shambhavi, the daily meditation practice that changed my life with its practical wisdom and started me on this journey. A very special thank-you as well to all my ALI cohorts for supporting me as I trudged through the deep snowy banks of the "messy middle," finding the courage to write my story. Also, much gratitude to John Kendzior, who opened his heart and heard my voice, and to Rosabeth Kanter, Jim Honan, David Woods, Rakesh Khurana, Jack Spengler, Bill Clark, Heather Hendrickson, Muriel Rouyer, and Marshall Ganz, who gave me the tools to craft this important message.

As you read through the pages of this book, you will get to know doctors, experts, and others who inspired and helped me pull together this information. I am especially grateful for my friendships with Ken Cook, William McDonough, Robert F. Kennedy, Jr., Terry Tamminen, and Durwood Zaelke, with Murray Clarke and Mary Cordaro, my environmental health heroes who started me on this path, and with Dan Schrag, who helped me see how critical the link is between climate change and our health. It takes a village to raise a child, but it takes an even larger village to write a book like this. I am not the specialist in this story; I am merely the messenger who is telling the story of the bravest and smartest people I know in the environmental health world. There are others I know who I was not able to include, but be aware that I am not done writing about this subject, and fear not: you will appear in an article or a blog somewhere authored by me in the near future.

I could not have written this book without thanking a few very important people. Firstly, my right arm and mini-me, Charli, who, with her quiet confidence, patience, hard work, and kindness, typed every word with love and humor. She never gave up nor did my editor, Joanne Tombrakos, who was introduced to me by my dear friend Agapi Stassinopoulos and wrote many of these chapters in tandem with me, both sitting across the room and across the country. She is a true Greek mother in every sense of the word and never let go of my hand until she felt I had said what I needed to say and in the way

I needed to say it. Also, thanks to our research team, Alexandria, Amanda, Kate, and Sandra, for all your hard work.

I am grateful for the unconditional love of my family, Tony, Alex, Colin, and Katie, for selflessly giving me up for hours, days, weeks, and months while I pursued my passion of writing down this story. I am especially grateful to Tony, who, despite difficult circumstances, took great care of our home (with the help of Irene) and of our children in my absence.

With love to my mother and father, who suffered through my rebellious years and never gave up on me and my dreams.

An immense gratitude to my girlfriends from all over the world, who have listened to me talk endlessly about this book. Thank you for never sounding bored or impatient.

A very special thanks to my best friend, a creative genius, who wrote me a birthday card from Winslow, Arizona, with two green hearts, which became the magic for this journey.

I want to thank Stephanie Krikorian, who introduced me to my agent, Joelle Delbourgo, who through persistence and belief in this message, found Denise Silvestro, who signed me as a new author the first week of her new job at Kensington. I had never written a book before, but working with Denise was such a gift that I could write another five books for her. Thank you, Denise, for loving this book from our first meeting and supporting me through the fires and floods. Also, thanks to Arthur Maisel and Jeffrey Robert Lindholm, for all your kind editorial comments.

And, with all my warmth, to John, for hugging me through every chapter of this book and for inspiring me with your passion to make the world a better place for all of us to live.

INDEX